LIFE
Learning Is For Everyone

Praise for LIFE: Learning Is For Everyone

"Readable, fast-paced, well written, and instructive—this book provides fascinating and important insight into the brilliant leadership, hard work, and innovative education program development of one individual. Donald Bailey, determined parent of a young man with a disability, painstakingly and competently built a network of people who put together the requisite pieces of support and commitment from within his state and beyond to create postsecondary education options for persons with disabilities in South Carolina. Anyone interested in disability, in education, in helping broaden the horizon of opportunities for young people exiting special education will be the wiser for having read this book."

Madeleine Will
Vice President of Public Policy
National Down Syndrome Society

"In *LIFE Learning is for Everyone*, Donald shares the story of honoring his son's vision of a different future for himself and how with perseverance, hope, and tenacity his family made that dream into a reality. His story shows that sometimes in order to help your children reach their potential you have to reach inside and meet your own. Donald demonstrates the power parents have to create new and better options for their children with intellectual disabilities and makes it clear that the first step in his journey was listening to his son's dreams and believing that they were possible. His efforts, initially on behalf of his son, have made a difference in the lives of many young people with intellectual disabilities throughout the state of South Carolina. In recounting his personal journey of hope, disappointment, and ultimately success, Donald demonstrates that all parents have the power to make change happen. He accomplished this by recruiting an impressive team of committed people to share in the mission of creating college options. These efforts will pay dividends for years to come for families of students with intellectual disabilities in South Carolina and throughout our country. I hope that every person, parent, teacher, and policymaker who reads this book sees in it a reflection of their own potential to make the dream of college into reality."

Meg Grigal, PhD
Co-Director, Think College
Institute for Community Inclusion
UMASS-Boston

"This book will inform and empower any American who cares about ensuring that young adults with intellectual disabilities get the postsecondary experiences they deserve to realize their potential. The process that occurred in South Carolina provides a viable blueprint to provide postsecondary options for any young person who is intellectually challenged, regardless of where they live."

Jim Rex, PhD
Former South Carolina State Superintendent of Education

"This is a must-read story of a family with an unwavering devotion to the education of their son. It seems as though every parent I talk to feels as if they are the only one on this educational journey. With a real-life happy ending, this book provides insight into one family's educational journey and the impact that the journey will have on generations to come for students with disabilities."

Edie Cusack
Director of REACH Program at College of Charleston

All proceeds from the sale of this book will be used to fund scholarships for students with intellectual disabilities enrolled in CTC-sponsored postsecondary programs in South Carolina.

LIFE

Learning Is For Everyone

The True Story of How South Carolina Came to be a Leader in
Providing Opportunities for Postsecondary Education to Young Adults
with Intellectual Disabilities

D O N A L D   B A I L E Y

as told to Ellen B. de Jong

iUniverse, Inc.
Bloomington

LIFE: LEARNING IS FOR EVERYONE

The True Story of How South Carolina Came to be a Leader in Providing Opportunities for Postsecondary Education to Young Adults with Intellectual Disabilities

iUniverse books may be ordered through booksellers or by contacting:

iUniverse
1663 Liberty Drive
Bloomington, IN 47403
www.iuniverse.com
1-800-Authors (1-800-288-4677)

ISBN: 978-1-4697-7927-0 (sc)
ISBN: 978-1-4697-7928-7 (hc)
ISBN: 978-1-4697-7929-4 (ebk)

Library of Congress Control Number: 2012902696

Printed in the United States of America

iUniverse rev. date: 03/08/2012

To all young adults with intellectual disabilities
who want to experience college life, be independent,
and have meaningful employment

CONTENTS

FOREWORD

Chances are if you are reading this book, you have a very personal reason to do so. Most who adopt a cause do so for personal reasons. My husband, Donald, certainly did. But there was something else that motivated him: a sense that it was absolutely the right thing to do. It was a matter of civil rights. On the one hand, I am in awe of what he has accomplished. On the other, I am not at all surprised!

Let me give you some insight into this man who changed the world of postsecondary educational opportunities for those with intellectual disabilities in South Carolina. I met him when I was in college, and we became friends instantly. As our ties strengthened over the years, we married and became parents of Carrie, who pretty well breezed through school and life, and young Donald, who was destined to struggle in many ways and was diagnosed at an early age with PDD-NOS. Neither Donald Sr. nor I knew much at all about developmental disabilities at the time. Little did we know how our world was to change!

As I got to know this amazing man, I became fascinated with figuring out just what made him tick, as I had missed his formative years. Donald was educated by virtue of his athleticism, with a football scholarship to the University of South Carolina. This experience shaped him in many ways. If not for football, he well may not have been able to go to college. I think that his college experience (football and the relationships he developed) had much to do with the man he has become.

Perhaps one of the strongest statements he ever made to me was in response to my question years ago about why he wanted to run for the Board of Trustees at USC. He simply said, "They educated me. It is my turn to give back."

He worked very hard to get there. He has never stopped giving back. Little did he know how those years would come back to help him with the journey he has outlined in this book. He brought people together. He generated energy and enthusiasm. He was never afraid to ask for help and support. He is not finished.

He continues to work for this population, to open up opportunities so that they may live meaningful lives and be contributors to the world around them. Rosa Parks would be very proud of him. I know I am.

May this book be a great inspiration for you.

Caroline Bailey

SPECIAL THANKS

To my best friend and wife, Caroline, for her continuous support of me and CTC. Without her, this effort would never have been successful. She has always been the person I shared all of my thoughts and ideas with before anything got done. She participated in all of the Task Force meetings, she shared her thoughts, and she has provided continuous encouragement and leadership.

She is and always has been a wonderful mom to our children—and now grandmother to our grandchildren. Thank you.

.

ACKNOWLEDGMENTS

Like so many families, we were motivated by our son to pursue opening doors that had not been opened in the past.

My son, Donald Jr., wanted to go to college like all of his peers. In South Carolina, there were no options available in 2005.

As a cognitively challenged young man, he didn't qualify to attend through traditional paths. The following people and more came together against huge odds to knock down the obstacles. The story to follow shows how we made history in South Carolina.

Many thanks to all the people we quoted and to those who shared their thoughts: the CTC Board, both past and present (Jane Breeden, Louise Morris, Delie Fort, Barbara Zaremba, Corky Carnevale, Debra Wilson, Caleb Fort, Peter Hughes, and Cate Cusick); the Task Force; and Erica Smith.

Ellen de Jong deserves many thanks for her countless hours of research and dedication. Without her interest, this would not have happened.

There are many more who need to be recognized and thanked. Forgive me for not mentioning everyone—the countless people who have lent their willingness to take action, their determined focus, and their persistence to this effort are true champions for all of South Carolina's students, as well as champions for all who are inspired by this effort to take action themselves. Thank you all.

INTRODUCTION

Somewhere along the way, it became obvious we were making history. Introducing the concept of allowing developmentally challenged young people to go to college in South Carolina had never been accomplished.

The time was right. There was a movement around the country we picked up on and pitched to the South Carolina legislature, families, and educators.

Almost from the beginning, we were confident of our success. Historically, South Carolina has not been recognized as a leader in education. This was different!

Educators, Board of Trustee members, college presidents, and the Superintendent of Education participated as willing partners to make this happen.

The following is my account of how it all happened. You will meet an amazing number of people from all walks of life who collaborated and made it happen.

Today, South Carolina is recognized nationally as a leader in postsecondary education for intellectually challenged individuals.

I am proud to share with you how this initiative came together to create five college programs in South Carolina. We hope you will be motivated to perhaps do the same in your state.

We have no secrets—we will be happy to offer any assistance along the way. Please visit our website at www.collegetransitionconnection. org or e-mail me directly at dbailes@bellsouth.net.

Chapter 1

WELCOME TO OUR WORLD

My name is Donald Bailey, and if you were to meet me in person, your first impression would probably be that I am a very gregarious, outgoing guy who enjoys life. And I am. But those who know me well know that when it comes to certain things—and especially when it relates to my family—I am also a very private person and very protective of those closest to me. Like many of you, I always considered myself to be an ordinary guy, never expecting my life to take me on a journey of enough interest and importance that people would ask me to make speeches or to write a book about it. You can imagine that no one is more surprised than I am by the demand for this book, and that no one is more gratified than I am by the hard-fought successes that are its reason for being. Looking back, the loss of privacy seems a small price to pay, and looking forward, it is my sincere hope that by making my story public, there are things that I can share with you that will inspire you in your own journey, whatever that might be.

If you are reading this book, you probably have an interest in the world of cognitive disability. Or perhaps you are interested in making things happen—taking on a challenge and refusing to accept a negative outcome. So let me start by saying that I am probably a lot like you. I did not begin this journey with any special skill set that qualified me to do what I did. Before my wife, Caroline, and I learned that our son has a cognitive disability, we knew almost nothing about the issues and challenges that this would bring to his—and our family's—world.

Likewise, while I have always tried to stand up for the things I believe in, I had never felt truly called to champion any cause. One simple but unexpected question from our son changed all that forever. Donald Jr. was a teenager when he asked, "Dad, am I going to college?" Knowing that he had the desire to go and that we certainly wanted him to be able to go, Caroline and I were extremely disappointed to discover that the postsecondary opportunities in South Carolina at that time offered very little hope that our son would, in fact, ever attend college.

So, when it all started, we were just a dad and a mom who, like most parents, dreamed of giving our children every possible opportunity in life. That innocently posed question from our son was a wake-up call, and from that moment on, I realized that the only way this was going to happen for our child was if we stepped up to make it happen. But I am getting a little ahead of myself. Before I go any further, let me first share with you a brief look back at the events that led up to that question so that you can better understand how and why it became my call to action.

In the early 1990s, the Bailey family was much like many American households. Mom (Caroline), Dad (that's me, Donald Sr.), big sister Carrie, and little brother Donald Jr. went about our day-to-day routines of school, work, extracurricular activities, and socializing. Because Caroline was, from day one, a very hands-on and involved mother, it was not long before she began to see aspects of young Donald's behavior that seemed outside the norm.

One of the very first things she noticed happened when Donald Jr. was about three years old: he just stopped responding to people. He would literally ignore them when they greeted him—no response, no acknowledgement. Not long after this behavior started, Donald Jr. began to develop an obsession with, of all things, *The Wizard of Oz.* Though this was definitely unusual at his age and, therefore, we were somewhat concerned, Caroline continued to do everything she could think of to foster and encourage positive, appropriate behaviors. When Donald Jr. started repeatedly drawing the Yellow Brick Road in chalk on our driveway, Caroline saw this as an opportunity to share time with our son in a fun artistic endeavor. So she and Donald Jr. got creative and worked together on a Tin Man costume—a funnel for a hat, cardboard covered in aluminum foil for the body, and a

2

papier-mâché ax to complete the outfit. Donald Jr. loved it so much that it was hard to get him to leave the house in anything else.

While it is not at all uncommon for a young child to get hung up on a favorite article of clothing for a time, it seemed to us that Donald Jr.'s insistence on wearing this costume to the exclusion of almost everything else was, again, outside the boundaries of what we were seeing with his peers. And there were other obsessions; although at first Donald Jr. didn't want to learn to wash his hands, he then moved into a period where he wouldn't stop washing them. And he was also incessantly brushing his teeth.

So what was going on with our son? Caroline and I wondered. As the red flags continued to appear, we decided it was time to seek professional medical opinions. Caroline videotaped Donald Jr. playing with a friend to document some of his physically awkward mannerisms and movements. We thought he might be having seizures, but an EEG proved this was not the case. Donald Jr.'s pediatrician called these random movements "tics," so our next thought was Tourette syndrome. That possibility was then also ruled out. It turned out that Donald Jr. could actually control these "spasms," and they were mostly a manifestation of nervousness or just plain social discomfort.

We continued to search for the cause of these unusual behaviors, and finally, after Donald Jr. had endured a battery of tests and interviews, Caroline and I literally sat on the edges of our chairs in the doctor's office. We listened in shocked silence to the diagnosis of PDD-NOS. What? We were clueless and more than a little afraid of what this ominous-sounding array of letters might mean—now and for the future of our son and our family.

PDD-NOS (pervasive developmental disorder–not otherwise specified), we were told, is within the autism spectrum. As it was explained to us, a child with this condition is like a computer that's missing a chip. Things are processed very slowly. Concepts that are not concrete are difficult to grasp. Difficult to grasp? That was something we certainly could relate to at that moment. And, just in case the specifics of the medical side of the diagnosis were not enough for us to try to deal with, some of the professionals who had assessed our son felt obligated to add a range of gut-wrenching predictions and recommendations, including the following:

"He will never finish school."

"Forget the social aspect—he will never have friends."

"You may want to consider institutionalizing."

And, the comment that really pushed us to our limits, forcing us to confront a raw emotional mix of frustration, anger, and pain:

"I would recommend you talk to a grief counselor—you really need to come to terms with the 'passing,' so to speak, of the child you thought you would be raising and to understand the reality of the son you actually have."

Presumably these experts were well-intentioned and thought they were helping us face reality by being painfully blunt. But when I look at the amazing young man our son is today, I am so grateful that Caroline and I were not, for one second, willing to just blindly accept all the negatives and go down without a fight.

Once we had recovered from the initial shock, we gathered together all the information we had been given and carefully looked at all the options we could consider for our young son. And then—secure in the knowledge that Caroline was my rock and that we were always, in all things, there for each other—I turned to my wife and said, "Well, if we don't try, we'll never know how much he can achieve, will we?"

And with that, we vowed to do whatever it took to give our son every opportunity to reach his full potential. Little did we know what lay ahead.

Chapter 2

SELF-ADVOCACY

If you have never awakened in the middle of the night in a cold sweat wondering what in the world you are going to do about _____ (fill in the blank with your own personal challenges), let me tell you, it is just plain terrifying. Concerns that may not seem overwhelming in the rational light of day somehow transform into unmanageable, insurmountable obstacles in the dead of night. *What should we do to help our son?* It was a deceptively simple, straightforward question that brought on many sleepless nights but, unfortunately, no equally straightforward answer.

As I said, our family had been abruptly and unexpectedly thrust into completely foreign territory by our son's diagnosis. Now, not only did we need to understand all the physical manifestations of PDD-NOS, but we also needed to learn about and help him deal with the emotional and social ramifications. We were totally committed to the process, so we plunged headfirst into this world called "Special Needs."

Yes, our son would have some needs that were "special" or different from other children, but he also had many, many needs that were just the same as all children: the need for love, the need for friendship, the need to be valued as a person. The love, at least at home, was not a problem. For Caroline and me, being parents was, and continues to be, a true joy in our lives, and we love both of our children beyond anything that words can convey. This is the foundation of all our efforts and, even in our darkest hours, our personal refuge of comfort and hope.

We embraced the new challenges in our world, doing whatever we could to help Donald Jr. as he struggled to find and establish friendships, providing support and comfort when his efforts made him an innocent target of public ignorance and fear. Our spirits may have dipped, and our hearts were often heavy, but our resolve remained strong. Though progress was slow and the all-too-infrequent victories hard won, we continued to look for new and better ways to enrich Donald Jr.'s life.

It is true that we are fortunate to be living in an era when the Individuals with Disabilities Education Act (IDEA) guarantees "free appropriate public education" (FAPE) to Donald Jr. and others like him. This federal law, enacted in 1990 and reauthorized in 1997, affirms that students who meet the eligibility requirements will have access to Individualized Education Programs (IEPs). In theory, this seems like a wonderful educational guarantee for children like our son. In practice, however, it does not always translate into quality programs or committed educators.

As in all professions, in education there are some teaching standouts—those individuals who go far beyond what is required and who inspire our children to believe in themselves and to not only achieve more, but to want to achieve more. These teachers, in our personal experience with Donald Jr., proved to be much more often the exception than the rule. Teaching, and especially teaching well, is a challenge, and the challenges for those educators who have chosen the area of Special Needs are exponentially greater.

To say that overseeing Donald Jr.'s education was an education in itself for Caroline and me would be the mother of all understatements. While Carrie progressed happily and seamlessly through her elementary, middle, and secondary years, each school year for Donald Jr., and sometimes each semester, brought new and often unanticipated issues. Ensuring that Donald Jr. was getting the appropriate amount of attention and motivation that would help him learn and grow, not just educationally but also socially and emotionally, was our goal. While a scant few of his school experiences were home runs for Donald Jr., most, despite our best efforts, left us feeling that the system had, to continue the baseball analogy, struck him out, or worse yet, kept him confined to the dugout, never even given a chance at bat.

Despite the frustrations and setbacks, we remained very hands-on throughout Donald Jr.'s school years. As we navigated our way through the options that were provided by our local public school system, we continued to search for other programs that might be a better fit and provide him with the structure he needed and, at the same time, give him the opportunities he deserved. We eventually found a program we felt really filled the bill. The one big problem: it was a thousand miles from our South Carolina home.

The Riverview School in Cape Cod, Massachusetts, seemed to have everything that Donald Jr. needed and everything that Caroline and I wanted for him. It is a residential school for students in their middle and secondary years who have learning, language, and cognitive disabilities. The student body is very small—fewer than two hundred students—and, as an added benefit, Riverview has a postsecondary education option that Donald Jr. could seamlessly transition to once he completed the high school portion of the program.

It seemed like the perfect package. But Massachusetts? Could we really let him go? We were concerned about the separation—as much for us, we had to admit to ourselves, as for him. And, after years of free public education, we were looking at a private school program that would cost close to $60,000 a year plus whatever we would end up spending to travel back and forth to Cape Cod. As before, we turned to each other to bolster our resolve, knowing that we were willing to do whatever it took if this was the right place for Donald Jr. And after an on-site visit and interviews, we determined that it was.

We were so convinced that Donald Jr. would thrive in this environment that we didn't delay acting on our decision. We pulled him out of our local school midyear and enrolled him in Riverview halfway through the eighth grade. With Carrie already out of the house and flourishing in her independent young-adult life, Caroline and I now settled into a pattern of spending every other weekend in Cape Cod. These trips were made as much to reassure ourselves that all was well with Donald Jr. as to provide him with the reassurance that Mom and Dad were still very much a part of his life.

And so it went: eighth grade—happily completed, ninth grade likewise, tenth grade—OOPS! Our smoothly flowing grand plan suddenly hit a major roadblock. Home for spring break of his sophomore year and relaxing with family at our favorite vacation hang-out, Donald Jr. suddenly announced he did not want to go back to Riverview the following year. He wanted, he said, to go to the local public high school, with more than twenty-five hundred other teens from his hometown. Wow! We really hadn't seen that one coming.

One of our main life goals for Donald Jr. has been to empower him—to teach him and give him the skills necessary for him to be a self-advocate. And now here he was, standing before us, calmly announcing what he wanted to do with the next couple of years of his life.

In the spirit of "Be careful what you wish for," Caroline and I now found ourselves squarely on the horns of a dilemma. Should we honor our son's wishes and support his self-advocacy, allowing him to return to an educational setting in which we knew from past experience he struggled mightily and which did not always successfully meet the needs of young adults like him? In the big picture, was this in the best interest of our child? And what about the years after high school? If Donald Jr. came home to finish high school, the transition to a postsecondary program at Riverview was no longer in the cards. And to our complete disappointment and utter amazement, we quickly discovered that our home state of South Carolina had no postsecondary options to offer our son—none. Parenting, as most parents will tell you, rarely provides us the luxury of easy decisions on issues that are very obviously black or white. Rather, it's the much more common gray areas that can truly confound us, and this one was a doozy.

Chapter 3

THE DREAM

After many late-night conversations and much soul-searching, Caroline and I decided we could not ignore our son's first steps toward independence. After all, wasn't this what we wanted for him? Wasn't our goal to see young Donald reach a point where he was in charge of shaping his own future?

So, when Donald Jr. returned to Riverview after spring break, he went knowing that we had agreed this would be his last year there, that his high school career would continue back home with us, at the local public school. Caroline and I made our final trip to Cape Cod that June and brought our son home with mixed emotions. Certainly there was pride, an enormous amount of parental pride. Without any outside influence, Donald Jr. had made a decision and had spoken up, letting us know how he wanted his life to proceed. This was a tremendous step forward on his personal journey to becoming a self-sufficient, self-advocating young adult, and we were both extremely pleased by the progress he was making. But was this big step forward destined to be followed by two steps back?

What we were now facing brought yet another emotion into play for us: fear. Specifically, fear of the unknown. Not so much about the coming two years—having navigated through the local school system in Donald Jr.'s early years, we felt we had the experience to deal with whatever we might encounter at the high school level. It was confronting and addressing the future beyond high school that brought beads of sweat to my forehead. Where would Donald Jr. go and what would he do once he "aged out" of the federally mandated guarantees for his education? Now that Donald Jr. was no longer at Riverview, we found we had lots of questions and absolutely no answers.

As Donald Jr. began his final two years of high school, once again at home with us in South Carolina, our family settled into a routine that was not unlike those of most families with teenagers. Donald Jr.'s life was filled with school and family activities, and Caroline and I worked hard to keep things on an even keel. But even as our son started his junior year, we could not ignore that there was a BIG deadline looming large on our horizon. We knew we could not wait until the end of Donald Jr.'s senior year to start planning for the future; we had to start now. But how to start? And what to do? We had no checklist to go by, no template to give us a framework within which to operate. Despite that lack of guidance, we were, as always, determined not to let our son down.

Marcia Bocim, who was working in my office at that time, remembers it this way:

> For years I had observed the drive that Caroline and Donald had to keep finding ways to help their son. They searched for and utilized every possible option for Donald Jr. and were totally dedicated to helping him work toward an independent life. When Donald Jr. expressed an interest in college—he wanted to go just like his big sister had—it was like a switch flipped in his dad's brain.
>
> That young boy's desire to do what his sibling had done and what his peers would be doing sparked a determination in his father that you just knew would make Donald Sr. unstoppable. His attitude about making it happen was, "Yes, we will. I don't know how yet, but somehow we will."

Caroline echoed those sentiments as she spoke to a group at the Citadel, a local military college, recalling the beginning of our journey:

> Donald had seen the postsecondary program in operation at Riverview while our son was there. When young Donald came back home and we began discussing what his future

might hold, my husband said to me, "We can do that here in South Carolina—I know we can." Right then, hearing that statement and knowing him as well as I do, I knew it was a done deal.

Once our son had come to us and asked if he would be going to college—and by the way, I immediately assured him that yes, of course, he would—Caroline and I were on a mission, with no time to spare. From that point on, every meeting, every social gathering, every chance encounter became an opportunity for us to find like-minded individuals and set the wheels of an as-yet-undefined plan in motion.

Again, Marcia's recollection: "Donald would network with anyone who would listen to him. He talked to everybody. The success of Donald Bailey comes from his never wanting to give up." She's right; once we had set the goal of establishing a postsecondary program in South Carolina in time for our son to take advantage of it, I was relentless, committed and determined to never give up. How could I? Why would I? We were fighting, at the very core of our cause, for our son's future. But before I jump into how things actually began to take shape, I would like to take a moment for a personal aside.

Like Marcia, there are a number of people throughout this book who say very complimentary and flattering things about me. I am humbled and, to be truthful, more than a little embarrassed by their kind words. But I would like to clarify a few things here at the outset because much of this attention, praise, and credit for what many call *my* success is undeserved:

1) First and foremost, without my wife, Caroline, nothing you will read about in this book would have been possible. As I stated earlier, she is my rock and the foundation of our family unit. If you were to ever make the mistake of referring to her as "the woman behind the man," I would have to immediately and emphatically correct you. Caroline is "behind" only in the sense of "behind the scenes." Caroline is, and always has been, central to every decision and every achievement, but, unlike me, she has the good sense to keep a low profile and stay out of the spotlight as much as possible. She is an amazing

11

wife and mother and every bit as driven and motivated as I have ever been.

2) I am a firm believer in the "power of one" and also believe it is the moral responsibility of each of us to step up when there are issues or causes to which we feel called. Equally important, however, when the task requires it, is finding and working together with a team of remarkable people and utilizing the unique skills of each person. This story is about just such a task and is very much about a *group* of people achieving success by working together. I may have been the catalyst, the motivator, and very often the spokesperson, but without a literal army of others who were crusaders for the same cause, this effort would have gone nowhere.

3) As most parents will tell you, achieving the unimaginable becomes possible when you are doing it for your child. I am completely unremarkable in that I have only done what parents everywhere have been doing for centuries: moving mountains so that their children will have a better life.

In 2005, Caroline and I were committed to testing the waters of creating a postsecondary educational program and doing whatever we could to get the word out, with fingers crossed that we could find others who were willing to join our fledgling grassroots effort. A couple of times that summer we hosted small, informal gatherings of residents of the greater Charleston area, and word of our intentions began to spread. A call from a group of parents in the Upstate area of South Carolina confirmed interest beyond our coastal community, prompting me to drive two hundred miles to the northwest for a meeting in Spartanburg. In addition to several couples from the surrounding South Carolina area, there was also a parent from Charlotte, North Carolina, who had committed to the three-hour round-trip drive just to attend my very bare-bones PowerPoint presentation. Caroline and I were encouraged and energized by the mounting evidence that a number of people wanted to be a part of this, even though none of us could yet envision exactly what "this" was or what it would become.

As I tried to get a true sense of what our efforts might entail, I knew I needed to look beyond the Palmetto State's borders for information and guidance. That effort took a huge leap forward when I finally got around to reading an e-mail I had printed out several weeks before but had left unread on a corner of my desk. Dr. Barbara Zaremba, Director of the Citadel's OASIS Program, which provides services and support to students with disabilities, had written me to bring my attention to an article written by Dr. Meg Grigal and Dr. Debra Hart. Little did I know that these were two of the preeminent and most well-respected authorities in the field of intellectual disabilities (ID).

At that time their names meant nothing to me, but the article caught my attention, so operating as I almost always do on the premise that if you don't at least try, you'll never know what might have happened, I picked up the phone and reached out to them. As it turned out, both of these very knowledgeable women were extremely gracious and enormously helpful in moving me along in my quest. In fact, many of the people mentioned in this book are highly educated, well-respected authorities in their various fields. Yet you might notice that I refer to all of them by their first names. No disrespect is intended; I am in awe of their knowledge and abilities. But because of the very personal nature of this journey, Caroline and I quickly found ourselves on a first-name basis all around. Each of these individuals has been so welcoming, giving, and willing to do whatever they could to help us further our cause that we have come to regard them all as friends.

Back in Charleston, at yet another gathering in the fall of 2005, a group of about twenty of us sat talking, waiting for a scheduled speaker who never showed. And here came my first big Aha! moment. It was one of those light-bulb moments that became a turning point when suddenly it was crystal clear in my mind exactly what should happen next. In this case, this unexpectedly agenda-less evening provided an opportunity for us to move from just talking the talk to taking a first step toward walking the walk. If we were truly interested in promoting change, it was time to get serious and get organized—it was time for us to form a board. Which is exactly what we proceeded to do.

There were four people on that original board: myself, Delie Fort, Jane Breeden, and Louise Morris. It was exciting to realize that we were a geographically diverse mix. I was down in Charleston, Delie and Jane were in the Upstate of South Carolina, and Louise lived outside of Charlotte, North Carolina. Our cause united us; we wanted our children to become happy, productive, contributing members of society. And in order to prepare them and give them the very best shot at achieving that, we wanted them to have postsecondary options that were close to home. Even for Louise's family in Charlotte, schools in South Carolina would provide a very real option.

Initially, each of the four board members committed to providing seed money, which, combined with an unexpected and very generous anonymous donation of $50,000, gave us the resources to begin to get down to business.

Jane Breeden recalls that early period: "We wrote checks and we gave our opinions as parents—and we were ambassadors for our cause. But from the very beginning, Donald was our Pied Piper." Adds Delie Fort: "We all recognized the clear need for postsecondary opportunities in South Carolina. As things stood, our children were destined to fall into a kind of 'no man's land' after high school. Donald and Caroline were very compelling, very passionate. You could tell they were committed to bringing this to the attention of those who should know—those who could help us make a difference."

So now we were on our way. What I would call our first "formal" gathering took place in early 2006 on Daniel Island, just outside of Charleston. About forty parents showed up, and we got right to the heart of the matter, addressing the possible outcome(s) that we were most interested in pursuing. There were some examples for us to consider—programs that were already operating in other states. Briefly, those options fell into three broad categories:

1) Dual-enrollment, which essentially provides for students to take classes on a college campus while fully enrolled at their local high school
2) Nonresidential, with students who have completed high school commuting from home to classes and activities on the college campus
3) Full residential, with students living together full-time in on-campus housing and participating in both academics and a wide range of extracurricular activities

There were pluses and minuses to be weighed and discussed with each of the three options. And, in addition to these existing models, there was another alternative, unique to our situation. Here is an excerpt from an e-mail I sent out prior to this gathering:

> I have some fantastic news to share . . . I met with two local developers at Daniel Island . . . To my amazement, they offered us 3,000 square feet in a new office project for our school . . . This is a perfect location . . . The best part, the project is expected to be finished in the Spring of 2007, just before we open in the fall. I am so excited, I just had to let you all know.

This was an amazing opportunity, and we agreed that it appeared perfectly suited to our plan. We were optimistic and enthusiastic because it seemed like, after a very short time at work, we were already well on our way. In reality, however, what was about to happen was proof of the old adage, "If it seems too good to be true, it probably is."

Chapter 4

THE START

"I had a very idealistic vision of how this concept would all just fall into place. I saw the community of Daniel Island embracing the program, providing housing in local apartments and jobs at local businesses. I thought they would just 'adopt' the program and go with it."

That's how Corky Carnevale, who by early 2006 was a member of our board, remembers his reaction to the Daniel Island option. And for a short time, that's how many of us thought it would come together. We had adopted a motto, "We can make it happen in September 2007," and it was looking like we had a good shot at achieving that ambitious goal. But for a number of reasons—logistics and finances not the least of them—this early plan very quickly developed some major problems. Fortunately for us, however, there was already some movement on "Plan B."

In March 2006, with Daniel Island now more of a question mark than a certainty, I outlined an alternative possibility to the group. This new concept would involve a partnership with three schools in the Charleston area: The College of Charleston, Charleston Southern University, and Trident Technical College. One of the major advantages of this approach would be the availability of academic and vocational training from established schools as opposed to having to staff a program from scratch. This would be a real money-saver for our organization and would allow us to focus more of our attention on the residential component, something we had decided was a very important element of our plan. This Plan B was brand new to the group and created some controversy among us. Because we were divided on the issue, it was decided that our Executive Committee should study the two plans further and make a recommendation to the board.

Key to our forward motion at this point was looking for ways to tap into the expertise and guidance of organizations that had already traveled this road and, as a result, could hopefully help us avoid some of the potential pitfalls. In the previous chapter, I mentioned Meg Grigal and Deb Hart. Besides sharing a wealth of information with us, these well-known and well-connected women also recommended we contact another big name in the field of Special Needs, Madeleine Will. Her name may be familiar, as Madeleine has maintained a high profile nationally for quite some time. Since the late 1970s, she has been advocating for the rights of individuals with intellectual disabilities in a number of capacities—as a lobbyist, as the Assistant Secretary of Education for Special Education and Rehabilitation, and in various positions with the National Down Syndrome Society (NDSS), to highlight just a few. At the time that I contacted her, she was serving as the Director of the NDSS Policy Center and was chairing the NDSS Transition and Postsecondary Education Project. Madeleine also put us in touch with Stephanie Lee, then a senior policy advisor at NDSS.

Through these two women and the Washington DC–based NDSS, I knew we had the potential for access to a staggering array of information, resources, and contacts, so I did not hesitate to ask Stephanie Lee what it would take for our group to be able to partner with them. With this in mind, I invited Stephanie to speak at our March meeting, and, after sharing a number of personal insights, she presented us with a formal proposal for a three-year partnership.

Within our group, excitement ran high, and we quickly voted in favor of this agreement that would provide assistance from NDSS on a broad range of analytical, advisory, and technical issues. That vote brought us to another major turning point in our journey. In just a few short months, we had managed to secure a relationship with a powerhouse mentor organization that could show us what had already been done in other locations and advise us on how to best define, refine, and accomplish our own goals.

Not unlike the transition we were hoping to facilitate for our children, this partnership with NDSS would help take us from our earliest incarnation as a somewhat naive group of well-intentioned parents to a more focused and informed organization with a clearly defined mission and goal. And along with these latest developments, our fledgling effort now also had an "official" identity. We had given ourselves a name: Charleston Transition College (CTC).

I can already hear what some of you are thinking. Well, that's great for him, but that's not something I could ever do. I could never secure those kinds of connections. But the truth of the matter is, if I was able to do it, you could, too.

My wife and I were both born and raised and went to college in South Carolina, just like we wanted both of our children to have the opportunity to do. I was typical of many college students in that once I got my degree, I sort of looked around and thought, "Now what?" So I spent a few years searching—both personally and professionally. Fortunately for me, by the time Caroline came into my life, I had figured out a lot of things. I knew what I wanted in terms of home and family, and I had found my niche professionally as well, building what has become a successful and thriving financial management business.

Caroline knew early on that she wanted a career in medicine, and, after completing her studies, began working in that field and has ever since. So, as two working parents with two children, we have backgrounds and a family life that are probably very much like your own. There was nothing special or unique in our backgrounds that prepared us for the roles in which we now found ourselves—advocating and working for change on behalf of our son.

While it is true that I do try to give my all when I commit to something, like everyone else, I have my personal strengths and weaknesses. I am not the guy to whom everything comes easily, and I am not a highly educated PhD. I like to tell people that the letters behind my name are PID—Parent of Intellectually Disabled. What I am is a guy who is motivated and willing to give 110 percent, but unwilling to accept "no" as the ultimate answer. The qualities that have helped me make things happen in life are characteristics that I think can help anyone in pursuit of a goal. If I were to summarize what

I believe has been most instrumental in bringing about my successes, it would be these three things:

1) **Willingness to Take Action.** Twice already I have mentioned my philosophy of "you won't know until you try." This applies to so many situations, no matter how daunting they may seem. Every great accomplishment started somewhere, with someone who decided to do something—to take action. And sometimes that someone needs to be you.

2) **Staying Focused and Objective.** It is important to view rejections or negative outcomes objectively. Keeping in mind that it is not you or your family or your personal situation that is being rejected helps develop a thick skin. You may or may not ever know why your plan, idea, or concept was turned down, but you must never lose sight of the fact there are many different ways to get to the same place—some are just more direct than others.

3) **Persistence.** Of course there have been times when I have felt down or discouraged, when things were not going as I had hoped—that's just normal human emotion. But I never let those feelings distract me for very long, and, most importantly, I never give in and give up. So if the first person or first avenue you try doesn't work out, regroup and go at it a different way or from another direction. You are going to read about that happening to us many times. And you already know that, ultimately, our persistence paid off. We did succeed—in a big way. Because we never gave up.

An interviewer asked South Carolina Senator John Courson, who, as you will see, had a hand in the success of our project, to characterize me and my approach. Here's what Sen. Courson said:

> Donald is likeable, persistent, and aggressive—without being abrasive. I would tell anyone, if Donald Bailey comes knocking on your door with a cause, there's a 99 percent chance that, in the end, you *will* be involved.

About Caroline and me as a couple, former South Carolina State Superintendent of Education Jim Rex characterized our efforts this way:

> Donald has that "failure is not an alternative" approach, and Caroline supplies the quiet assurance that "we know what we are doing—this is the right thing." And their parenthood gives them credibility and authenticity.

As I've said: we were motivated, coming from a place of parental love, and we just wouldn't take no for an answer. And we were willing to take action. So the question now facing our group was what exactly was the course of action we were going to take?

Chapter 5

THE PLAN

So here was our situation in the spring of 2006: in my early enthusiasm I had sold people on a plan that was looking less and less viable with each passing week.

Searching for guidance from those with hands-on experience, I was referred to Susan DiFabio, who proceeded to give me a very frank reality check. Susan had worked in Vermont at Landmark College, a school specifically for students with learning disabilities. Landmark is a two-year program with a residential option for its student body of about four hundred fifty students who come from forty states and several foreign countries. Susan remembers well her early discussions with Caroline and me:

> Donald's enthusiasm and grand vision were commendable and inspiring. But Donald is not an educator and seemed unaffected by the governance systems and complexities within higher education—typical obstacles that go hand-in-hand with this type of educational innovation. His vision would call for a paradigm shift, and the details of his ideas were in need of refinement.

Susan laid out for us what would be involved from the education standpoint and also touched on the potential political and legal ramifications of our ambitious plan. When Susan finished with us, the rose-colored glasses through which we had gazed at Daniel Island were definitely off. At that point, CTC made the decision to abandon our original plan and pursue the option of some type of partnership

21

with the three established Charleston-area schools. But this was not a unanimous vote, and, as a result, we lost a few members of our group. These individuals had committed to a plan they believed in, and the new developments were moving in a direction they felt they could not support. Fortunately, however, most of the people who had agreed to work with us were willing to regroup, embrace the new approach, and see where it might lead.

Susan's comments also put something else on our to-do list: we needed to see for ourselves the day-to-day reality of programs that were already up and running in other parts of the country. And with NDSS in our corner, we now had an "in." NDSS had already helped put a program in place at George Mason University in Northern Virginia and was in the process of doing the same at The College of New Jersey (TCNJ) just outside of Trenton. So, soon after our vote to move forward with a new plan, several CTC members, led by Madeleine Will and Stephanie Lee, went on a fact-finding mission.

We spent two days on TCNJ's campus soaking up as much of the real world experience as we could. We brought new insights and even greater enthusiasm (if that was possible) back with us and shared what we had learned with our fellow CTC members. As we began to refine our ideas for a partnership with the local colleges, we drafted a mission statement:

> CTC works with select colleges and universities in South Carolina to design, create, and fund transition and postsecondary school opportunities for young adults with intellectual disabilities.

We also worked to more clearly define the goals for CTC. Our four main goals, which have continued through the years to be our focus, are the following:

1) To make it possible for students with ID to have the opportunity to experience college life
2) To enhance the social life of these young adults
3) To give them the tools to prepare them to live independently
4) To help them develop skills and to aid them in finding meaningful employment

Kind of sounds like what parents everywhere want the college experience to provide their children, doesn't it? But for us, this was ground-breaking stuff. In generations past, parents of children with special needs never dared to imagine that this might one day be a reality for them. But we had seen the reality in other places, and we were bound and determined that it would become one for our children in South Carolina as well. And sooner, rather than later.

There was another element of our grand plan that Susan DiFabio had addressed, and we knew that if we wanted to get on the fast track to success we needed to give this our immediate attention. It was time to start enlisting the support of as many people of power and influence as we could muster.

We started close to home with a man who certainly fit that description—Charleston Mayor Joe Riley, who at the time was in his eighth term as the city's top official. When asked about our first meeting with him, Mayor Riley had the following reply:

> Donald and Caroline coming into my office gave me a gift. Their passion and emotion were evident, yet they were able to clearly present their idea—an idea I found profoundly important and compelling. Their presentation was a light-bulb moment for me . . . I thought, "This makes so much sense. Why hasn't this been done already?" I was happy to be a part of it and to do whatever I could. But all you had to do was listen to them and you knew they were going to get this done.

With Joe Riley in our corner, we had the support of the City of Charleston behind us. And the mayor kept abreast of developments by sending a representative to each of our Task Force meetings. This had been another step forward for us—the formation of a Task Force and a Steering Committee to help guide our actions. Our Task Force was a group of about thirty, made up of some members of CTC, Madeleine Will and Stephanie Lee from NDSS, and representatives of various groups from around South Carolina that were interested in helping us achieve our goal. One of those representatives was Dana Reed from the Office of Exceptional Children within the South Carolina Department of Education.

We also recruited the Director of the Center for Disability Resources (CDR), Dr. Richard Ferrante. The CDR, which is housed at the University of South Carolina School of Medicine in Columbia, is one of sixty-seven University Centers for Excellence in Developmental Disabilities (UCEDD) located around the country. NDSS had urged us to contact Richard, and we were fortunate that he agreed to serve, not only on our Task Force, but on our Steering Committee as well.

"I needed to be there to represent our center," Richard recalls, "and there was also the issue that Donald Bailey has this ongoing auditory processing problem. He simply cannot understand the word 'no.' I really had no choice." Richard also connected us with a number of other people at organizations who would be helpful to our mission: Dr. Beverly Buscemi, State Director of the Department of Disabilities and Special Needs, and, from the all-important world of vocational rehabilitation, Larry Bryant, Commissioner of the state's Vocational Rehabilitation Department, and Barbara Hollis, the department's Assistant Commissioner.

Vocational rehabilitation—known within the world of ID as "voc rehab"—was a crucial element of our overall plan and, more specifically, our goal of aiding students with finding employment following their postsecondary experience. As Richard likes to say, "We will all know that we have truly made progress when we are talking about careers for young adults with disabilities rather than just jobs." The employment component was, and always will be, so important to our goal of helping these young adults lead productive lives of as much independence as they are able to achieve.

But before we could work on helping them transition to employment, we needed to help them transition to college, so first things first. Our focus was now solidly on how we could make this plan a reality in partnership with the three local schools: the College of Charleston (CofC), Charleston Southern University (CSU), and Trident Technical College (TTC). Dr. Frances Welch, now Dean of the School of Education, Health, and Human Performance at CofC, was the department chair at the time and was involved with our concept from day one. "After several meetings and much discussion," says Fran, "representatives from the three schools came up with a cooperative plan under which Trident could provide the courses, Charleston Southern the residential portion, and the College of Charleston, with its campus

24

in the heart of downtown, would be where the social component took place. This was the basis for the proposal that was submitted to CTC."

In November 2006, CTC's Steering Committee held a teleconference to discuss this proposal from the colleges. The consensus was that it was a good starting point, but that there were a number of red flags and stumbling blocks. Here is a paraphrased summary (taken from the minutes of that teleconference) of some of the major issues that we agreed needed to be addressed:

> The Request for Proposal (RFP)* clearly asked the colleges to come up with a high-quality, sustainable program that would allow the students to accomplish the following:
>
> - become a real part of the college community
> - attend various classes (with support in regular classes)
> - participate in extracurricular activities
> - know other students, and
> - feel a sense of belonging
>
> *The entire document can be found in Appendix A.
>
> The proposal that has been submitted fails to meet the Task Force's original vision in a number of ways:
>
> - recruitment of students is focused at the local, rather than regional, level
> - the proposal does not address the "typical day" or how students would be included in meaningful ways on a daily basis
> - the proposal fails to be truly inclusive in that it calls for a substantially separate program where students are driven around together in a van and are visibly differentiated from other students
> - assessment and documentation of progress is focused on CTC as a program and does not address these areas for individual students
> - the logistics of the three-college arrangement creates an unnecessarily large and expensive bureaucracy.

Regarding this last issue of collaboration, it was suggested that the proposal could be streamlined by decreasing the number of colleges involved—and that, in fact, it would be easiest to work with just one school. However, since all three schools were participating in good faith, we could not just summarily dismiss any one institution. The three colleges had applied jointly, so we needed to continue to deal with them jointly.

It was suggested that a small contingent from our group meet with the college representatives to explain our concerns and help them better understand our vision and the importance of certain elements that were missing from this proposal. Inclusion was such a core issue for us, and we were extremely disappointed at the glaring lack of that element in their plan. We definitely needed to address whether these colleges could realistically see this happening on their campuses.

During this teleconference, we also discussed the possibility of suggesting to the colleges that, based on the level of expense and logistical support required with this three-college plan, it would be more streamlined and cost-effective to work with just one school with the potential to expand to other institutions later on. Maybe they would be receptive to this . . . but we really didn't know.

What was obvious from this discussion was that we needed to get the schools—or at least one of the schools—to bring their vision more in line with ours. We still had a lot of hurdles to jump, but the dialogue had been started and we were anxious to keep our momentum going. Our stated goal of opening a program in August 2007 was looking less and less attainable, but we knew it was far more important to get the details of the program right than it was to adhere to some arbitrary timeline. A follow-up meeting with the school representatives was set, but what happened next was something none of us could have envisioned or anticipated.

Chapter 6

THE CHALLENGES

CSU Community 'Shocked' By Charges
Board chairman: 'We regret' $10M in scholarship funds
were turned over to Parish firm
Post and Courier, Saturday, April 7, 2007

"It seemed like a good idea at the time. Turn over $10
million in Charleston Southern University scholarship funds
to Parish Economics LLC, the investment company of Al
Parish, the school's trusted, flamboyant economics professor
with a reputation for shrewd money management."
Post and Courier, April 7, 2007

"Charleston Southern University may suspend hiring and
building projects in the wake of accusations that its star
economist lost or stole $10.6 million of its savings."
Post and Courier, April 11, 2007

"Failed economist Al Parish was sentenced Thursday to 10
years in prison for securities fraud, the maximum penalty he
could get in state court for an investment scheme in which
hundreds of investors lost an estimated $66 million."
Post and Courier, September 19, 2008

In January 2007, Charleston Southern University abruptly pulled
out of the three-college partnership. Though the university was not
specific at the time about their reasons for withdrawing, within a few

weeks the local newspaper would provide daily details of a major economic drama unfolding on the campus. It was clear there was no hope of reviving any interest in our program with CSU.

Without the housing that was to have come from CSU—Trident had no dorms and, as is the case at most colleges in the twenty-first century, dorm space was already at a premium at CofC—one of the cornerstones of our concept—inclusion—was out the window.

To our great disappointment, after months of hard work, Plan B collapsed around us like a house of cards. If ever there was a time when I needed to be guided by some of those characteristics I mentioned in chapter 4—staying focused and objective and being persistent—this was it. In fact, I did not have the luxury of time to do anything but forge ahead, as I was already on the agenda to testify before the General Assembly in Columbia in just a few weeks to request funds for our program.

So here was another defining moment: a turning point in our journey that showed what we were made of. A testament to the inner strength of those who were part of our effort, we rallied yet again, with CTC members pledging their continued support and our Task Force and Steering Committee members standing firm in their commitment to help us reach our goal. As we began work on a new approach, I think we were all silently hoping for proof that the third time would be the charm!

As we progressed through late 2006 and the first few months of 2007, our quest became less linear, branching out in a number of different directions, all of which required personal attention at a variety of times and places. Multitasking became the order of the day. While talks with the three colleges were going on, I was also meeting and talking with local and state politicians and legislators and maintaining contacts at the various state agencies with whom we now had relationships. In addition, South Carolina had just elected a new Superintendent of Education with whom I was anxious to meet. As it turned out, our proposal was right up Dr. Jim Rex's alley.

"I ran as a reform candidate, and I sincerely wanted to bring about systemic change," remembers Jim Rex.

> The proposal that Donald laid out for me gave me a bully pulpit—the perfect opportunity to expand awareness in

South Carolina of how many young people could benefit from a program like this. There is a mistaken perception among many that K-12 is more than enough education for children with intellectual disabilities when, in fact, the learning process is lifelong for all of us. Without question there should be postsecondary opportunities for these young people.

Jim's wife, Sue, who was a professor in the area of special education for twenty years at Winthrop College in the northern part of South Carolina, also lent us her support. "What I admired so much about Donald and Caroline was that even though they were very upfront about the benefit to their son, you saw very clearly that they believed all young people with intellectual disabilities deserved this opportunity.

Having Jim and Sue on our side was a big feather in our cap, but we were at the point where, in addition to very vocal support from prominent, influential people, we needed fiscal support from our state government. We had managed to raise $300,000 through our own efforts, and now it was time to make our plea to the state for additional monies to help get our program off the ground. I had laid the groundwork, meeting with and talking to Rep. Harry B. "Chip" Limehouse and Sen. John Courson, as well as with others in the state legislature. And now I needed to put my shoulder into it and try to move our request for funding forward.

"Donald explained the need for this program," recalls Rep. Limehouse, "and, having known his family for a long time, I knew that if it was something that he had this deep of an interest in, then this was a worthwhile thing. So I made the arrangements for him to present his proposal at a subcommittee hearing."

On January 31, 2007, just a couple of weeks after the three-college plan fell apart, I made our case for the funding of $300,000 before the Higher Education, Technical, and Cultural Subcommittee of the House Ways and Means Committee. (Testimony in its entirety can be found in Appendix B.) I presented the subcommittee with pertinent statistics about unemployment rates for the population with ID and the resulting economic burden on society and stressed the positive impact that even one year of postsecondary education

29

has on the likelihood of these young people finding jobs and living independently.

Perhaps most powerful and compelling of all, I brought with me two young people with ID who would be able to benefit from our program and asked them to tell the legislators what it would mean to them personally to have a postsecondary experience. For all of my calling and lobbying and working behind the scenes, I firmly believe it was those young people and their heartfelt personal testimony that sealed the deal for us. "From that point forward, the initiative has received broad-based support in the legislature," says Rep. Limehouse. And, in fact, we got approval from the full House on the first vote.

Even as our request for funding was working its way through the House, CTC was brainstorming a way to breathe new life into the search for a home for our program. We had started with an RFP to the three Charleston-area colleges, but we now agreed we should throw those geographic limitations out the window and think on a bigger, broader scale. We would send all the colleges and universities in South Carolina—there were about seventy at that time—an RFP, and we would invite them to an all-day gathering. We would bring in experts in the field of ID and representatives from existing postsecondary programs to speak and share information, and we would offer technical assistance to those institutions wishing to apply for consideration.

Mirroring our commitment to inclusion in our own program proposal, we would be inclusive in our invitation to participate—no one would be able to say they didn't know about it or hadn't been offered the opportunity to learn more. This was pretty much our fourth-and-long Hail Mary. What if we gave this "party" and nobody came?

Chapter 7

THE ROUNDTABLE

There was much to do in advance of this gathering, and we felt renewed excitement and energy as we considered the possibilities and opportunities that might arise as a result of it. We began to spread the word several months prior to the event through an e-mail that read, in part, as follows:

> Please save the date of June 21, 2007, for a Roundtable on Postsecondary Opportunities for Students with Intellectual Disabilities.
>
> The Roundtable is being sponsored by:
> Charleston Transition College (CTC), National Down Syndrome Society (NDSS), South Carolina University Center for Excellence in Developmental Disabilities Research (UCEDD), and the South Carolina Developmental Disabilities Council (DD Council) . . .
>
> The purposes of the Roundtable are to
>
> 1) expand interest in postsecondary options among key state leaders;
> 2) provide technical assistance to colleges and universities interested in applying for the RFP;
> 3) generate collaboration with key state agencies; and
> 4) provide an opportunity for Task Force members to gain and also share knowledge.

We had already lined up Jim Rex and Larry Bryant to speak to the group. We were hoping to secure commitments from other state officials and experts in the fields of education and ID and were working to confirm presentations from existing programs in other states.

As we were discussing those model programs, we decided it would be beneficial to make another on-site visit. Madeleine Will, along with the NDSS Research Manager and project director for New Jersey, Erin Geller, facilitated our return trip to The College of New Jersey and then to nearby Mercer County Community College, site of another program started with help from NDSS. Caroline and I, along with Richard Ferrante, were joined by Jane Breeden, Delie Fort, and Louise Morris—our very first board members and still very much involved and committed—on this New Jersey trip. Our goal was to further educate ourselves on the true day-to-day issues and details involved in running programs at both a four-year residential college and a two-year community college. As an added bonus, we came home with a commitment from both programs to present at our upcoming Roundtable.

With so much going on, we found ourselves needing to delineate areas of major focus; it just wasn't possible at this point for each of us to give our full attention to all developing areas. I was already deeply involved in the legislative aspect, working to secure the much-needed funding, so that was where I felt I could do the most good. Stephanie Lee and Richard Ferrante were leading the effort to get all the details of the Roundtable worked out, and various CTC members continually stepped up whenever and wherever they were needed in order to try to ensure our ultimate success.

All this work, of course, was accomplished in our "spare time," as we all also had full-time responsibilities at our places of paid employment. Granted, NDSS was providing their assistance under a paid partnership agreement, but Stephanie, who is based in Washington, had made numerous trips to South Carolina and had more people and groups than just ours vying for her time and attention. With each passing day I had a greater and greater appreciation of these people—not just people associated with CTC, but people in classrooms and in families and in volunteer groups and in paid organizations who focus on improving the quality of life for individuals with ID. These are some of the most giving and caring people that you will ever have the great fortune to encounter. Caroline and I had witnessed it throughout our son's life, and we saw and felt it everywhere on this unpredictable journey toward a postsecondary program.

As work continued on the preparations for the upcoming Roundtable, I was frequently on the road to Columbia. While the House had already approved our funding request, we still needed to get it through the Senate. John Courson was then, and continues to be, the Chairman of the Senate Education Committee. In his own words:

> Getting involved with a new program is not something I take lightly. But this program was very much in line with my core beliefs about our responsibility as a state. South Carolina has an obligation to assist those with intellectual disabilities in whatever ways possible. We should and must do whatever we can to assist these students in obtaining as much formal education as possible to give them the tools to become more productive members of society.

As fate would have it, the Senate vote on our proposal was scheduled for June 21, the same day as the Roundtable. I know proper cell phone etiquette dictates that phones be turned off in presentations and group settings, but I already had plans for a back-up battery and loud ringtone that day. There was no way I was going to risk missing a call about our financial fate.

So, with cell phone close at hand, I arrived at the Marriott in Columbia on that sunny June day with Caroline and newly graduated Donald Jr.—yes, our son had just finished high school! It had now been two years since Donald Jr. came home from Riverview and about a year and a half since Caroline and I first began our quest in earnest to guarantee him a postsecondary opportunity in South Carolina. Donald Jr.'s experience at our local public high school had been, on balance, a fairly positive one, thanks mostly to a few truly caring teachers.

So, when Donald Jr.'s high school years were nearing their end, we had asked him if he wanted to stay a little longer at Wando High, as was an option for him under IDEA. (The law guarantees that young adults with ID may attend high school until age twenty-one.) Donald

Jr.'s response to this question was a very pointed, "Why would I want to do that?" Why indeed? Walking into that Roundtable meeting with our son now out of high school and with still no postsecondary options in the works at South Carolina colleges, I knew this day would be another major turning point in our journey.

We had a very impressive group of presenters on hand—recognized experts in the field of ID at both the national and the state levels. Many of the names you have already read about were there: Madeleine Will, Stephanie Lee, Meg Grigal, Debra Hart, Richard Ferrante, Jim Rex, and Larry Bryant. To give details of and answer questions about programs already in place, representatives of The College of New Jersey and Pennsylvania State University were on hand. (Mercer County Community College had to cancel at the last minute due to illness.) And even though the Roundtable was being held on a workday, CTC was well represented by Corky Carnevale, Susan DiFabio, Delie Fort, Jane Breeden, and Louise and John Morris, to name a few. Speaking of CTC, since we had expanded our search beyond the Charleston area, we realized we were in need of a name that would reflect our new approach. So, going forward, we would be known as College Transition Connection.

And now, the all-important news on attendance by colleges . . . drumroll please . . . we had twelve colleges send representatives to the Roundtable that day, indicating their interest in responding to our RFP. This translates to more than 15 percent of the total that had been invited. Of course, we would have loved for it to have been more, but it was a very good start. Things were really looking up. And then my cell phone rang.

Chapter 8

FUNDING

Remember that feeling as you walked to the bulletin board in the hallway of your high school to see if you had been given a role in the play or made the cut for the varsity team? Or walking to the mailbox to see if you were going to get the little envelope or the big packet from the college you really wanted to go to? That old familiar stomach-turning mix of hope and fear, anticipation, and anxiety was immediately upon me as that first ring echoed from my jacket pocket.

I hurried to the privacy of the hallway and pushed the green button to connect the call. And with three little words—"You got it!"—I was transported to Cloud Nine.

"It wasn't a difficult sell," Sen. Courson recalls. "Both the Senate Education and the Senate Finance Committees passed the funding request simultaneously." This truly was a red-letter day and I could barely contain my excitement as I waited for just the right moment to announce the news to all in attendance at the Roundtable. Spontaneous applause erupted when I shared this latest development, and I couldn't help but feel that this vote of confidence, in the form of the Senate concurring with the House in their approval of our funding, would boost our credibility with the colleges in attendance and improve our chances of getting real, solid interest in aligning with our program.

Here again was undeniable reinforcement for exercising those traits I mentioned; we had taken action, remained focused, and been incredibly persistent . . . and we were finally reaping tangible rewards. All we needed now was a commitment from some college or, as we hoped, *colleges* that would be willing to take a leadership role in bringing postsecondary opportunities to a very deserving segment of our young adult population. We had pulled out all the stops, and at the end of the day, the state's two largest universities declared their intention to respond to our RFP.

The University of South Carolina, with full-time undergraduate enrollment at about seventeen thousand students in 2007, and Clemson University, with just over thirteen thousand undergrads, both stepped up and committed to submitting proposals in response to our RFP. "Frankly, the way Donald orchestrated and managed this 'campaign' could not have been better," remembers Dr. Dennis Pruitt, head of Carolina's Office of Student Affairs since 1983:

> He displayed what I call "professional persistence" and was a true driving force. I think everyone from the university president on down had gotten a call from Donald and was aware of what he was trying to do. It was both a personal endeavor and a move to benefit society. It wasn't that I was skeptical, but I could see the amount of work that would need to be done, and it would definitely put a strain on our disability office, where resources were already stretched pretty thin.

With that in mind, Dr. Karen Pettus, Carolina's Director of Student Disability Services, was one of the first to be given the opportunity to look at our request: "I was asked to write the response for why we *shouldn't* take this on. Frankly, I couldn't find a reason not to."

Sharon Sanders at Clemson University had this to say about those early days: "It is an intuitive thing that we need to do more to support students with ID. But ID encompasses a very wide range; people have varied expectations and a lot of questions. I knew that if we could get the Clemson community to understand what this program was all about, they would be supportive."

The two schools were eager to explain this cutting-edge initiative to faculty and staff and to lead South Carolina into a new era of education reform. They each had until mid-September 2007 to flesh out the details of their programs, get their plans and ideas on paper, and submit them to CTC. We answered their questions and concerns and provided whatever assistance they needed in preparing these documents, all the while anxiously anticipating the results.

And while we waited, up sprang another speed bump on our road to success in the form of a veto of our funding by then-governor Mark Sanford. Fortunately for us, the House and Senate voted to override the governor, the money from the state was given the final green light, and CTC's plans were quickly back on track.

For the Bailey family personally, the unexpectedly slow pace of our forward progress meant we were now faced with another decision. Donald Jr. had finished high school and had made it abundantly clear that he had no desire to go back for a fifth year. There was nothing yet in place in South Carolina, and he was, like most kids his age, anxious to move on. Caroline and I had reviewed materials from numerous programs around the country during our research, and we discovered one we liked that would keep Donald Jr. a little closer to home than Riverview had.

The Horizons Program in Birmingham, Alabama, as their website informs, "offers a nondegree postsecondary program specifically designed to facilitate personal, social and career independence for students with mild learning disabilities." That had a familiar ring to it. We had a family discussion and, with Donald Jr.'s approval, enrolled him in Horizons for the fall of 2007, with the plan being that the following fall he would be able to transfer back home to a program in South Carolina. But having been on the brink of success—or so we thought—twice before, we knew better than to make Donald Jr. a promise we (still!) might not be able to keep.

Chapter 9

SUCCESS!

"We were prepared to move out of state," recalls Katie Burgess. "We had begun homeschooling when Bryann was in the fourth grade, and as she moved into her teen years, we started to look for postsecondary opportunities. There seemed to be nothing in South Carolina. And then, a chance invitation to a meeting brought Donald Bailey and his incredible vision for an educational opportunity in South Carolina for Bryann into our world." Bryann was one of the two young people I mentioned who spoke to the General Assembly about what the opportunity for a postsecondary experience would mean to her. She also gave her first-person testimony at the Roundtable.

Bryann is an incredibly poised, well-spoken young lady with an interest in, and talent for, music. "Because of Bryann's strong interest in studying music, particularly voice and piano, we were thrilled to learn of the wonderful Berkshire Hills Music Academy in Massachusetts," Katie says. "We were all so impressed with the program when we visited the school, but Bryann ultimately decided that it was too far away from home and that she did not want to attend a school that was only for students with disabilities." With Carolina and Clemson announcing their intentions to establish these programs within their collegiate offerings, the Burgess family, like the Baileys, began to feel real optimism about providing the type of college experience their child was hoping—and asking—for.

For the colleges, starting a program like this from scratch was a double-edged sword. On the one hand, it was a wonderful, once-in-a-lifetime opportunity for them to "make it their own," to tailor and customize their program to their unique campus. On the other hand, with all the different departments and individuals who needed to be on board with the program, it was not always easy to get everyone to accept, to agree, and to commit to work together to ensure success.

"For some people, there continues to be an element of 'Why should I care?'" says Louise Morris. Knowing that this attitude still plays a part in some people's perceptions, there are certainly parallels to be drawn to the Civil Rights movement in this country. And, in fact, that comparison had been brought up to many of us at CTC throughout this journey. Louise continues, "This initiative was an evolution of what was coming out . . . and our culture was right for it." Adds Richard Ferrante: "We don't have a regular ed world and a special ed world, we have a world in which disability is a fact of life." Jim Rex agrees, "If we really love our children, we must care about the other children who are in the world with them, because they don't just share a childhood, they share a future, as well."

As the weeks progressed, it became clear that working through the details of a pilot program was hitting some snags on the Clemson campus. All our hopes were now on Carolina. "Donald had met with resistance early on from some of the top people at Carolina," recalls John Palms, president of the university from 1991-2002:

> I had a personal interest in this program because a member of my wife's family has some special challenges. I also saw this as something we as a state should be supporting. As past president of USC, I knew that this program would add value for all the students, not just those with intellectual disabilities, and so I was happy to do what I could. I assisted Donald in establishing some important contacts at a number of universities and attended some key early meetings in support of the plan. It was an honor for me to play that role. But make no mistake about it, it was Donald who bird-dogged and stayed on top of it all the way.

That "bird-dogging"—that persistence that has worked for me so often—paid off again, as Carolina came through for us with a fully outlined response submitted by the September deadline. Was everything perfect? No. Did we feel we could work with it? We were certainly willing to try. So we scheduled an on-site visit to the campus in Columbia on October 1 and called for a teleconference of the Task Force two days later.

The discussions by the Task Force were comprehensive; we examined and analyzed every aspect of Carolina's proposal. Some of the major points with which we were very pleased included the following:

- commitment from the Dean of Education for working to build support for the program within the university
- expressed intent to develop a model program that could be replicated on other campuses
- a shared vision of the importance of inclusion
- faculty support and commitment to having students involved as peer mentors
- Disability Services support and commitment to finding social mentors

Much of the feedback regarding areas of concern focused on admissions. We did not want to eliminate possible participation by large segments of the population we were hoping to serve by imposing overly specific or overly rigorous admissions criteria. There were also some questions about the proposed length of the program—would it definitely be a two-year program, or would there be flexibility to continue into a third and fourth year? And what exactly was the age range of those who would be eligible?

The Site Visit Committee reported to the Task Force that it had met with those who had actually put the proposal together and had also talked with the Dean of Education, Dr. Les Sternberg. "We had seen it all on paper," says Stephanie Lee, "but this was so important. We wanted to be face-to-face to see, hear, and feel that there was real commitment there." Dean Sternberg definitely got what we were working toward: "I thought it sounded like a really great idea. I am in favor of any well-thought-out program that gives kids with cognitive disabilities the opportunity to prove low expectations wrong."

After hearing the Site Visit Committee weigh in with its unanimous recommendation of approval of the proposal, I called for a vote by the

Task Force. Did we feel that the proposal submitted to us by Carolina had enough of what we were looking for? Could we on the Task Force endorse and therefore recommend that it be accepted by the CTC board? Richard put it very well when he said, "Let's not let the perfect be the enemy of the good—I'm not aware of any perfect anything." And so we voted unanimously to recommend that Carolina's proposal be accepted, contingent upon satisfactory discussions on the areas of concern outlined above. By early November our questions had been asked and answered to our satisfaction by the university. It was decision time—time for the board of CTC to vote. And what a feeling that was. We spoke as one voice in a unanimous mandate to approve the proposal, to award funding to the Carolina LIFE (Learning Is for Everyone) program, and to usher in a new era in education reform for the state of South Carolina.

It was truly a grand slam. We were bringing it all home . . . not just a program in South Carolina, but a program at South Carolina's flagship university and a program that would finally fulfill that promise we had made to our son years before. The next year he would not have to go out of state; he could attend my alma mater.

It was a very proud moment on so many counts. But for the time being, we had to keep it under wraps and contain our excitement, and that, as you can imagine, was not easy. We were all under a strict "gag order" because we didn't want word to get out until we were ready to make the official announcement in conjunction with the university. Finally, after weeks of NOT being able to say anything and with the Clemson proposal still on hold, on January 16, 2008, it was my distinct honor and privilege to announce the very first grant of $155,000 to the University of South Carolina.

Announcing the Grant at The Inn at USC

The first Carolina LIFE students would be arriving on campus in August, and Caroline and I had every intention of being there in the dual roles of program supporters and parents of an incoming student.

Chapter 10

CAROLINA LIFE

Our victory was huge, but so was the reality of what we now faced. Carolina LIFE would be the first such program in the state and was certain to be watched very closely by other institutions, both in and outside of South Carolina. It was critical that this pilot program be top-notch—and here we were, already more than two weeks into 2008, announcing to the world that Carolina would be enrolling its first students in this program in August.

We had just a few months to get the details of the program fully ironed out so that applications from eligible students could be solicited and assessed. In addition, the grant money that the state had awarded for the program was not to be administered as a single lump-sum payout. Rather, it was to be apportioned over three years' time—$55,000 the first year and $50,000 for each of the second and third years. The program proposal we had received from Carolina outlined a two-year program with plans to expand to a third and then, hopefully, a fourth year. The future of this program, and possibly others to follow, was riding on the successful implementation and administration of this inaugural year of Carolina LIFE.

"When an innovative program like this is proposed, there is often resistance, because it is not seen as part of the 'core mission' of a university—it is viewed as an 'add-on,'" explains Dennis Pruitt:

> At the schools that have taken on these types of programs, typically there have been two key elements that have led to their success: an advocate and resources. Obviously, the advocate was Donald Bailey; he was a subject matter

expert and the driving force. As that driving force, he also secured the necessary resources, including state funding as well as some of the Bailey family's own money. While this was, on one level, a personal endeavor, it also is something that benefits society, and Donald had a contingent of supporters. My only concern was: Can we make this a quality experience and provide it in a safe environment?

Karen Pettus, who, as you may recall, was one of the first to see and evaluate the proposal, echoed Dennis's sentiments: "I think everyone on this campus wants the program as a whole to succeed and the individual students to be successful, but there is concern about the students' safety. Legal issues arise, as well; in some cases the fear of a lawsuit heavily influences decisions." Also, Karen points out, the plan for Carolina LIFE was not to be simply an extension of what was in place in South Carolina's secondary schools:

> This would be an opportunity for these young people to truly transition and grow—to learn to make decisions for themselves, to begin to speak up and self-advocate, to develop self-confidence. This would be a place where they would be allowed to say "no" because, if we want them to develop critical life skills, we have to honor their moves toward independence. And we need to support them doing their own work, because if we don't, we are sending a message that says, "You are not good enough."

From the beginning, Karen found herself wearing a number of hats with respect to Carolina LIFE. As she explains it, hers is something of a balancing act, helping parents understand the goals of the program and bringing their perceptions and expectations more in line with those of the administrators and others at the university. "I try to find common ground, because I have always felt the program was a good idea for the students—for *all* of the students."

Not just high profile, this would be what Dennis called a "high maintenance" effort requiring enormous dedication and commitment. The early work on Carolina LIFE was shared by Dean Sternberg, Karen Pettus, and Dr. Alisa Lowery, who was in the Department of Special

Education at that time. When Alisa left Carolina in the summer of 2008, we were very much under the gun, and Les asked the Head of the Department of Special Education, Dr. Kathleen Marshall, if she would take responsibility for the Carolina LIFE Program "for a year."

"That's the way it was presented to me," remembers Kathleen. Teaching full time, chairing the Special Ed Department, and being involved with two doctoral leadership grants, Kathleen, like Karen, was already stretched thin in terms of time and resources. "While other start-up programs have had up to a year to prepare, we did not—and there was no model within the state. I did visit George Mason, but that was a different type of program than what we proposed. The individualized program we wanted to offer came with different challenges." Despite what she admits were "a lot of volunteer hours" and many situations that required "a lot of patience," Kathleen calls this work "a labor of love." (And, by the way, that "for a year" commitment became two, three, and then four years. Kathleen continues to be involved with Carolina LIFE, though the leadership has been taken over by Dr. Anthony "Tony" Plotner.

With Karen already working on the Disability Services side of the plan, Kathleen focused her energies on the financial and academic aspects. "I was trying to save as much money as possible procedurally, and also working on academic content. Karen and I knew who to talk to and how to move things forward. We didn't have the luxury of time; we needed to get things done." And they did.

"We wanted the application process to be as much like the process for other students as it could be," Karen explains. "The prospective Carolina LIFE students completed the same application that all non-degree-seeking students complete and returned them along with three letters of recommendation and transcripts/IEPs from their high schools." Donald Jr. was away at school in Birmingham when the applications were mailed out. So for Caroline and me, it was more than a little challenging to assist him long distance with the required forms to make sure they were submitted on time.

Perhaps the greatest frustration for all of us working to make Carolina LIFE a success was the cost of the program. Tuition was $8,000 per semester, plus other fees. Back then, students were not eligible for loans, grants, or federal aid. Fortunately, that has changed in ways I will explain shortly, but in 2008, this severely restricted the pool of applicants. "There were several students who wanted to apply but did not because of the cost of the program," recalls Karen. "We talked with several parents who were very disappointed and a few downright angry because they could not afford tuition and didn't have a way to finance the education for their child."

In the end, five students applied to Carolina LIFE. All the applicants were in-state residents, as the program was not yet equipped to handle the residential component. Knowledge of the program had come mostly through word of mouth from a teacher who had become aware of the program or from someone who was familiar with CTC. Awareness of postsecondary programs for the intellectually disabled has been one of our biggest challenges, and that summer we had had almost no time to formally market and create buzz about this new opportunity. Getting the word out continues to be a major focus of our time and effort at CTC because parents need to know that a diagnosis of Special Needs for their child is not a reason to cancel plans for a college fund. Options are available and more come into existence every year—it is a very exciting time in this area of educational reform!

Back to the Carolina campus where Donald Jr. and four other students were interviewed and completed a writing assignment on how attending Carolina would help them accomplish their goals. As with the admissions process for mainstream students, "no one was guaranteed a spot," says Karen. Again, the intent was to make the experience as much like everyone else's as they could. "It was a little nerve-wracking for some, but it would not have been nearly as exciting for the students if they had just 'known' all along they were accepted."

Like all the other applicants' families, the Bailey family waited anxiously for the e-mail notifying us of the school's decision. In the end, three students were admitted that first year because that was the most the school felt it could support in this highly individualized program. There was jubilation in the Bailey household and in two others, but for those of us who were also interested in the program's long-term success and accessibility to families at all economic levels, our own happiness was tempered by frustration at the limitations already being presented because of the program's cost.

In order to help make the program more affordable and therefore available to more prospective students, Kathleen led the effort that resulted in Carolina LIFE being recognized and approved for Pell Grant funding eligibility. In addition, Richard Ferrante reports that the state's vocational rehabilitation department has become the first in the country to fund students attending a nontraditional program like Carolina LIFE. And Les Sternberg, who has retired from his day-to-day responsibilities at Carolina, remains very involved in fundraising for Carolina LIFE. Les works tirelessly to raise awareness of the program and to bring in donations to The Frank and Frankie McGuire Endowed Scholarship.

Frank McGuire was a former basketball coach at the school whose son, Frankie, had multiple disabilities. During the 1960s and 70s—a time when many felt the disabled should be institutionalized or kept from public view—Frank proudly showed his love for and devotion to his son who was always courtside in his wheelchair, cheering on his dad and their beloved Gamecocks. I would recommend you take the time to go to http://youtu.be/sZQv42lMn7A and watch the story of the McGuire family and a man who lived his life in a way that was the very definition of the word "inspirational." I guarantee it will brighten your day.

And speaking of a day-brightener for the Bailey family, and I'm sure the two other students' families as well, seeing our child on the Carolina campus on that sunny August morning—well, there really are no words to accurately describe how Caroline and I felt. We were witnessing the culmination of so many hours of work and dedication from so many amazing people who had joined us in this quest; we were both proud and humbled. And the good feelings continued because this accomplishment came with a terrific ripple effect as peers, mentors, faculty, and students around the campus began to interact and bond with our children.

And in my mind, I reanswered that question that had started it all: "Dad, am I going to go to college?"

"Son . . . you're there!"

Chapter 11

CLEMSON LIFE AND COASTAL CAROLINA LIFE

Whatever happened with Clemson, you might be wondering? That is actually another very interesting story. Because at one point, we thought we had lost Clemson forever as a potential home for a LIFE program.

"What makes you think people around here are interested in this type of program?" That's the question that Sharon Sanders was hearing. Sharon was one of the early champions of our cause on the Clemson campus, and, as she recalls, it was a hard sell in the beginning. "We are in rural South Carolina and incomes are not high. Basically, the school thought no one in the area could afford the program." And there was skepticism and concern on other fronts, as well. "It is a slow educational process with those unfamiliar with cognitive disabilities," explains Dr. Joseph Ryan, an Associate Professor in the School of Education who wrote the grant application for Clemson LIFE.

Clemson officials obviously needed to be convinced, and we at CTC decided we would go to their campus and try to show them that the LIFE program could succeed in their area. Having no idea of what the turnout would actually be, we coordinated with Joe and Sharon to set up a site visit and informational meetings at Clemson on March 4, 2008. Again, if you are keeping track of the timeline, this "wooing" of Clemson was taking place concurrently with developing the program that had already been funded at Carolina. With Carolina already in the planning stages, we had momentum—and a long history of a healthy rivalry between the two powerhouse schools—working in our favor to bring Clemson on board.

As it turned out, March 4 was a rainy, miserable day—not at all the type of weather one hopes for when trying to get people to turn out for the types of gatherings we had scheduled. Madeleine Will and Stephanie Lee joined us that day at a luncheon to which all of the special education coordinators and disability agency representatives within a fifty-mile radius had been invited. We ended up speaking to, and answering questions from, a total of twenty-nine attendees, a very respectable turnout in this part of Upstate South Carolina on a rainy day.

Our evening event was geared toward parents. "They issued a tornado warning at six o'clock that evening. We thought we were doomed," recalls Sharon. "But more than seventy people showed up—some who had driven as much as one and half hours to be there." If Clemson needed convincing that there was interest in their community, here was irrefutable proof. This was an Aha! moment all around. Not only did people show up, but many who were there that night also offered to assist Clemson in whatever ways they could in this endeavor.

"Once the university understood, they were so supportive," says Sharon. Joe adds, "It became a win-win for the campus at large." As with Carolina, there were still issues to work through, primarily relating to tuition costs, housing, and community perceptions. "When people in the area started to hear about the program, the concept was so new that many wanted to know if the students who would attend the LIFE program would be taking spots away from the students in Clemson's mainstream undergraduate population," says Sharon. Everyone associated with the program worked to correct these types of misconceptions and educate people about the true nature of the program. "We really felt like trailblazers!" Sharon says.

A month after the on-campus informational meetings at Clemson, Sharon came to our next CTC gathering to explain in detail the university's plans for a LIFE program. And when Sharon finished her enthusiastic presentation, we once again voted our unanimous approval for funding—this time for Clemson LIFE. The award, which was contingent only on our receiving funding for a second year from the legislature, would give Clemson its first grant money in July with a planned start-up the following January.

We were now two for two. We were on a roll and loving every minute of it. And we knew we were really making headway when the next school to come on board actually *reached out to us first*. A buddy of mine called to let me know that one of his business clients had heard what we were doing and wanted to talk to me. That gentleman turned out to be the Chairman of the Board of Trustees for Coastal Carolina University. We had a telephone conversation during which he wondered aloud: "Why can't we have one of these programs?" And with that, the process was set in motion.

The idea of bringing the program to Coastal's campus was quickly and enthusiastically embraced. The school saw it as a good fit with the part of their mission that is focused on bringing education to underrepresented segments of the population. As had Carolina and Clemson before them, Coastal responded to our RFP and then we, as usual, scheduled our on-site visit. We were met with a very impressive—and very visible—show of support from the top down.

Among those present at that meeting were the university's President, the Provost, the Chairman of the Board of Trustees, and the Dean of Coastal's Spadoni College of Education. "This was the most welcoming institution of higher learning I have ever been to," recalls Richard Ferrante. They were obviously very motivated and their timing couldn't have been better: we actually had the money to fund them.

It all fell into place—and with the added bonus of bringing more geographic diversity to our postsecondary offerings. We had Clemson in the Upstate and Carolina smack in the middle of South Carolina and now Coastal Carolina, which, as its name implies, is located on the east coast just outside of Myrtle Beach and very close to the border with North Carolina.

By now we were getting to be quite skilled at working through our points of concern with interested colleges, and once we were comfortable with the details of Coastal's proposal, we approved their funding. The first check for Coastal LIFE was presented to them in January of 2009 with students expected on the campus that fall.

From left: Gayle Disney and Emma Savage-Davis of Coastal Carolina, CTC Board Members Delie Fort and Jane Breeden

Three programs, each incorporating special attributes coming from their individual campuses. Three programs . . . and counting.

Chapter 12

WINTHROP TRANSITION COLLEGE AND COLLEGE OF CHARLESTON REACH

"It has been one of the most fun things I have done in a long time." That is the assessment of Dr. Caroline Everington, Associate Dean of the College of Education at Winthrop University, when asked about her involvement with the school's postsecondary program for students with ID. As I mentioned, each of the LIFE programs has its own unique attributes, but they do share the common characteristic of being exclusively managed and overseen within a single campus. Winthrop's program differs at its core in that it is what is called dual-enrollment. Students in this program are also enrolled in a local high school and the program is jointly administered by the individual high school districts and Winthrop University. The program has a different structure and a different name—Winthrop Transition College. Its affiliation with CTC also took a different route than the others before it.

"Donald had approached the school several years ago, but the timing was not good," recalls Caroline. "I always had it in the back of my mind, but in the meantime we had two local school districts come to us, looking for a way to bring the college experience to some of their students with ID." These young people were eighteen to twenty-one years old and their peers had graduated and moved on, yet, as I mentioned before, they were still entitled to attend high school under the IDEA. But the high schools felt their curriculum was not meeting the needs of these students.

Dual enrollment was a different approach than what we had experienced before, but we did not want to close any doors.

Unfortunately, by the time Caroline had found support on campus for one of our programs and Winthrop was able to formally respond to our RFP, we no longer had the money to fund them. We were very fortunate in that the legislature had continued to approve funding for CTC's ongoing education-related initiatives, but another South Carolina college (their story in a moment) had beaten Winthrop to the punch and had become the fourth school to receive a grant award.

Still, Winthrop undertook its own effort to work in conjunction with two local high school districts, Rock Hill and Fort Mill, to expand the experiences available to their students with ID. Winthrop is arguably the best teachers' college in the state, known for turning out quality educators. And, as it turned out, having young people with ID on campus, even for limited amounts of time, was a learning and growth experience for all involved. "The transformation in our traditional students was amazing—the change of perceptions was phenomenal," Caroline reports. "The first academic classes we placed students in were Elementary Education Methods courses. We were concerned about the reception from the classmates; before long they were fighting to have the students with ID in their group." Many of these young adults with ID had never been in an inclusive classroom before, but, Caroline says, "I insisted that this would not be a 'social placement.' They *will* have assignments and tests and presentations. And we also wanted each of them to be involved in some kind of club."

Because of the way this dual-enrollment program is structured, Winthrop does not charge these students tuition, and, as such, there is no income stream to the university. So, with their own pilot program already in place, Caroline did not give up on the pursuit of a grant from CTC, which we were finally able to award in the summer of 2010.

"It has gone so much better than I ever thought," Caroline says. Program Coordinator Michelle Foster adds, "I've seen it affect the whole campus. We have a wide variety of mentors, and they are not all education majors. I see the students with ID interacting with the entire campus, not being treated any differently than any other students." And the experience has been so positive from the high schools' perspective that a third school district, Clover, has approached Winthrop about participating. Though *Charleston* Transition College (remember that's what we first called ourselves?) couldn't quite find its niche, *Winthrop* Transition College definitely has.

And speaking of Charleston—remember the school that I mentioned that applied for and got the grant that Winthrop was seeking? It was the College of Charleston, and with their response to our RFP, we had truly come full circle. Also, geographically, we finally had a program in the Lowcountry, close to home for the Bailey family, though Donald Jr. was already happily settled in at Carolina. But what was it that brought CofC back into the fold?

"With the original vision, students would have lived on one campus, taken classes on another, and participated in activities at a third. It would have been difficult—the transportation challenges alone would have been significant," says Dr. Cynthia "Cindi" May, Professor of Psychology at CofC. "If it had been implemented as first planned, it would likely not have been successful," Fran Welch adds. But even as Carolina and then Clemson and then Coastal were planning and implementing their programs, "Donald remained tenacious throughout. He had the vision, and he wanted it in Charleston," Fran remembers.

Two things happened that gave us the foothold we needed on the CofC campus. First, there was impetus from a CofC alumna who was working at one of our local high schools. The program she was involved with, the Bishop England High School Options Program, to quote their website, "provides students (from a wide range of cognitive abilities) an opportunity for inclusion in regular classes where everyone is enriched by the experience." This woman was passionate about her students having access to a local postsecondary program that was similarly committed to inclusion, and she wanted that program to be at her alma mater.

She began working with Cindi May, and there was our second, and very powerful, motivator. Cindi's interest was both professional and personal. In 2003, the May family had welcomed a beautiful baby girl named Grace who was born with Down syndrome. In June 2006, Grace was diagnosed with leukemia and passed away just six weeks later. When I first approached Cindi about helping us get a program up and running at CofC, it was just too soon after losing Grace. Though it continues to be hard to talk about, after the passage of some time Cindi says, "I felt called to be involved. When Grace was born it was important to me to find the best way to educate children with intellectual disabilities. Research has shown that inclusion produces the best results, so inclusion became my goal." Being involved with the pursuit of a postsecondary program at CofC was one of the many ways Cindi has been able to honor Grace's memory and to send an important message to Grace's four siblings (Grace was one of the May family's triplets and there are May twins as well), to the world of education, and to society as a whole.

"I was very familiar with what was going on at Bishop England, and I had also flown to Seattle to see an Options program there that has been in operation for twenty-five years," says Cindi. "The impact on all the students is huge. So all along I was aware of what was going on at other schools." Though Fran is Dean of the School of Education, Health, and Human Performance, she felt our program warranted a broader commitment than just from the School of Education. "This was a campus-wide program, and it needed a campus-wide team," Fran says. "The College was expanding—we now had beds and the space to accommodate this. Cindi coalesced the people of the plan, and I knew the process to get the approvals."

It was a star-studded event on the CofC campus on February 4, 2010, when we formally announced the awarding of a grant to the REACH Program. (CofC had opted not to call their program LIFE in order to avoid confusion with a scholarship by that name that is known throughout the state of South Carolina. REACH stands for Realizing Educational and Career Hopes.) On hand to congratulate the College and to celebrate the launch of this new program were many of the names you have already read about here—State Superintendent of Education Jim Rex, State Representative Chip Limehouse, Charleston Mayor Joe Riley, and NDSS representative Stephanie Lee. Also present were College of Charleston President Dr. P. George Benson and Charleston County School District Superintendent Dr. Nancy McGinley and a number of CTC board members. Besides me (I always get the fun job of presenting the oversized check!), Caroline, of course, was there as were Jane Breeden, Corky Carnevale, and Delie Fort, along with prospective students with disabilities and their parents. These young people were fortunate indeed to now have the REACH Program, with Cindi and Fran at the helm, and four other diverse and rewarding postsecondary options to explore in South Carolina.

Chapter 13

GRADUATION AND THE NEXT STEPS

Donald Sr., Caroline, Donald Jr., Carrie
May 7, 2011

Graduation Day. I'm sure I don't have to tell you how emotional this day was for all of us. But what you can't tell by looking at our smiling faces is that this photo almost didn't happen. We almost missed graduation. Our home is about two hours' drive from the Carolina campus, so of course we had allowed plenty of time to get there—this day was too important to have anything go wrong. But we hit an unexpected bump in the road, figuratively; *literally*, we hit a pothole that resulted in a flat tire and a delay that almost ruined the day. What got us through it with good humor was, once again, a question from Donald Jr.: "If we don't make it to graduation in time, does that mean I have to go back for another year?"

Just like when we had asked him if he wanted to spend another year in high school and he assured us he did not, Donald Jr.'s tone of voice let us know that he did not want to go back. As much as he had enjoyed his time at college, like many of us when those four years come to an end, he was ready to be out of school and on his own. When asked by a reporter what his major at Carolina had been, he said, "I majored in independent living." And now he was ready to put what he had learned to use and make a life for himself beyond the college campus.

So, as you can see by the photo, we *did* make it to Columbia in time for Donald Jr. to don cap and gown and walk across the stage at the Colonial Life Arena. Dr. Harris Pastides, president of the university since 2008, shook his hand and, knowing where Donald Jr.'s family was sitting in that sea of proud relatives, looked our way and gave us a thumb's-up. Though Harris was not directly involved in bringing the Carolina LIFE program to the university (he took office the same month the first LIFE students arrived on campus), he has, as president, declared himself "unadulterated in my support of it." He and his wife have personally invited all the students to events in their home, and it has meant so much to Caroline and me that on a campus with more than twenty thousand undergraduates, Harris never failed to remember and acknowledge Donald Jr. whenever their paths crossed. Harris knew the significance to us, and to the university, of Donald Jr. making history as the very first Carolina LIFE graduate.

Later that month, history was also made at Clemson, where six students became the first group of Clemson LIFE graduates. What we had dreamed of, hoped for, and worked toward was now a reality, actually far exceeding our original dream. We now had not one program but five, and the state of South Carolina had gone from the back of the pack to a leadership position in providing postsecondary educational opportunities to young adults with ID.

On each of the campuses, these programs continue to evolve. "We are constantly honing our program," says Winthrop's Caroline Everington.

Joe Ryan at Clemson sums up a feeling shared by all: "Each program has its own flavor, its own niche," And, he predicts, "As the programs age, they will differ even more."

If you are interested in more in-depth information on the programs as they are today, I have included a summary of each of the programs and contact information in Appendix C.

"We are still pushing uphill right now," Joe says, and Tony Plotner at Carolina concurs: "We are still learning, breaking down misconceptions, getting people on board." Tony was hired in 2010 to take over as the Director of Carolina LIFE. He and Joe also agree on the topic of future expansion—neither of them wants their student population to get too large. "We are like a small family," Tony says, "and from year to year, I see the growth in each individual student."

Helping the students discover their passions and achieve their potential is a core mission of the programs, and the schools' faculty and staff work very hard to enable and empower each of them. At CofC, Edie Cusack, who was hired as the Director of the REACH Program, likes to tell each of her students, "You are like a tree, growing and spreading your branches, and I am like the roots—hidden, but always there to offer strength and support." But there has been no hiding from the public eye for Edie or anyone else affiliated with REACH Program, following this very exciting announcement in October 2010:

College of Charleston
receives $2.3 million federal grant

Charleston Regional Business Journal, October 25, 2010

A $2.3 million federal grant will be used to support a four-year program to help adults with learning disabilities have a college experience at the College of Charleston. The U.S. Department of Education awarded the grant to help fund the Realizing Educational and Career Hopes: Foundation, Augmentation, Replication program.

"We view this as an extraordinary opportunity for the college to establish itself as a national leader in inclusive education and to promote inclusion not only at the postsecondary level, but also at primary and secondary levels as well," said Cynthia May, a professor in the psychology department at the College of Charleston.

"This award by the Federal Government sets CofC up as a model—the premier program in the state. Others from around the country will come to observe the REACH Program," says Richard Ferrante. "What is happening in Charleston is cutting edge—they clearly understand the concept of inclusion."

It seems somewhat ironic now to look back and realize that *not* getting the concept of inclusion was one of the things that doomed that first proposal from the three Charleston-area colleges. How amazing it is to realize how far we have come.

"Progress comes only with determination and a belief that change can happen," says Madeleine Will. "People gather around a person like Donald Bailey not just because the idea is strong, but also because they come to believe that this person is going to be there until the goal is reached." Yes, I was there, Caroline was there, and many other equally committed members of CTC were there. And yes, the goal of establishing postsecondary programs has been reached. But, as we've achieved one goal, another has come into focus. What about life *after* college? "There is no finish line," says Louise Morris, "and these young people will take what they learn out into the world and try something on. Maybe it works, maybe it doesn't. But life is a journey, for them and for all of us."

Helping them figure out what their next step on that journey might be is a priority for each of the programs. "Beyond life skills and social support, we also need to teach our students how to find and keep jobs. Transition and employment are important elements, and we continue to work on developing relationships that will lead to internships and apprenticeships for our students," says Carolina's Tony Plotner. At Clemson, Joe Ryan says, "We have done really well with placing our students in on-campus work environments. Now we need to get more external locations to offer work that will be challenging enough for them."

Donald Jr. had come to college with a variety of work experiences already under his belt. He had summer jobs during high school at Lowe's, at the local KAO campground, and at the gift shop at Patriots Point, home of the USS *Yorktown*. At Carolina LIFE he continued to add to his employment résumé, working with the maintenance crew on campus, helping out at the Strom Thurmond Wellness and Fitness Center, and completing an internship at the YMCA. While he could point to a good mix of work experiences, the economy in 2011 made the job search tough for new graduates of any program. And many employers are just not open to the idea of giving adults with special needs the opportunity to prove themselves. Fortunately, the Charleston County Park and Recreation Commission (CCPRC) is not one of those narrow-minded employers. "We have a firm commitment to diversity," says Tom O'Rourke, Executive Director of CCPRC, "and that includes not just race and gender but also disabilities. Our staff is dedicated to making sure that our offerings AND our employees mirror the diversity of the population we serve."

Tom and I had known each other casually for many years. As Tom recalls it, it was after some conversations with Edie and Cindi at CofC and also some of the staff at the Citadel who work with students with ID that we actually began to talk in earnest about what Donald Jr. might be able to do within the local park system. "It was like a light bulb clicked in my mind," Tom says, "and I saw clearly how I could use Donald Jr. to demonstrate to people locally, nationally, even internationally the advantages of hiring people with special needs."

I did not take offense at Tom's suggestion to "use" our son; I knew he meant it as a good thing, making Donald Jr. an example of the positive impact on the workplace in the same way that Donald Jr. had become an example of the positive effects on a college campus.

So it is with great pride that I can now report that not only is our son living successfully on his own, a few blocks away from Mom and Dad, but Donald Jr. also has a job. He works twenty-five to thirty hours a week at the moment (with the holidays approaching) at the Holiday Festival of Lights, a three-mile-long display of lighted holiday decorations in one of our local county parks. "This stretches him," Tom says:

> He's driving at night, which scares the heck out of his father! But Donald Jr. has shown us that he has the traits to be successful. I don't mean the skill set—that's our job to teach him. But he has the desire and the work ethic. He arrives on time, and he does his job well. He is perfect as an employee, and I want other employers to see that. We have two other individuals with special needs who have been working for us for years—and I can tell you they are truly invisible to the rest of the staff in terms of their disabilities. They are just part of our team, which is a really wonderful, dedicated group of people.

> I'll tell you why Donald Jr. is only working part time. It's not because he can't handle full time. It's because we are treating him like we treat everybody else, and we have LOTS of newly graduated young people who want to work here. It is incredibly hard to get a full-time job in our agency because everybody loves working here and nobody ever leaves. So you really have to work your way in, and Donald Jr. is doing that just like others his age are doing.

"We are all so different in so many ways. But everyone deserves the right to try—as long as someone has the ability, they should not be denied that right," Tom asserts, adding that there are lots of different things Donald Jr. now wants to try.

Like many young people just starting out, he is working at finding his niche. And Tom and I both had big ideas about what kinds of jobs he should be trying. We kicked around lots of different plans, and when Tom took them to his staff, they looked at him and said, "But have you asked *him* what he wants to do?"

"I had to admit that I hadn't," Tom says, laughing, "and that that was probably a good idea. As it turned out, what Donald Jr. wanted to do was nothing that I had been thinking of."

Not long after that experience, Tom had another "suggestion" from his staff that also turned out to be another Aha! moment for me. Aware that Tom and I had been doing a lot of brainstorming and planning for Donald Jr.'s future, Tom's team made this request: "Get out of the way. And while you're at it, get his father out of the way, too." Good advice. Because Donald Jr. is out there and doing great on his own. He knows that we are always here for him if he needs us, and we are very happy that several times a week he drops by for a meal or a visit.

But Caroline and I know that like most people his age, Donald Jr. wants to experience life on his own terms. And that is what this journey has been about—doing everything we could to prepare him, to provide the opportunities, and, ultimately, to allow him the freedom to do just that. It's his life, and the time has come for us to just get out of the way and let him live it.

Chapter 14

REFLECTIONS

Don't Just Take My Word for It . . .

I wouldn't want to end this story without sharing with you some of the thoughts and feelings of other parents and students who have first-hand knowledge of the programs you have read about and of young people with ID. I think they provide additional important impressions and insights.

Parents

"This is a dream come true for us. We never dreamed that big. Shame on us, but we never did."

—Parent of a CofC REACH Program student

"(My daughter) loved the program from the very beginning. The professors here believe in her."

—Parent of a Carolina LIFE student

"Here's what my son said to me: 'I am capable—just give me the opportunity. I want to be somebody. I think this is the program for me.'"

—Parent of a CofC REACH Program student

"This program has offered my daughter a chance to develop skills and independence. She has gotten opportunities here that she never would have had otherwise."

—Parent of a Clemson LIFE student

"He wanted to go to college in the worst way. And now he wants the Program Director's job!"

—Parent of a CofC REACH Program student

"These kids desperately need them [postsecondary programs]. We couldn't have made it any better than it was."

—Parent of a Clemson LIFE student

"My son is making some real friendships—this is huge for him."

—Parent of CofC REACH Program student

Students

"I don't want to live my life depending on other people. I want to stand on my own two feet. Being able to take care of myself and one day live on my own has been a goal of mine. I want to be able to give back to my community. I can have self-respect and live with pride in myself."

—Carolina LIFE student

"I'm excited about it [having the college experience] and sometimes really nervous. I haven't figured out what I want to do with my life. I want to find that in college."

—CofC REACH Program student

"When I first got there, I was completely nervous. I didn't expect to be with so many awesome kids."

—Clemson LIFE student

"It's fun to be on campus. There are boys and girls that I have met here that I will keep up with all my life."

—Carolina LIFE student

"I'm now living on campus, and it's really exciting!"

—Carolina LIFE student

"Embrace your disability. Let that be your power; let that be
your platform."

—CofC REACH Program student

Roommates

Donald Jr. had a different roommate each year at Carolina. What
follows are observations from two of those young men.

Wayne Hiott

"He felt like it was a victory—a vindication of sorts." That's how Wayne
Hiott, Donald Jr.'s lifelong friend, characterized Donald Jr.'s reaction
to being able to attend the University of South Carolina in the LIFE
Program. Wayne is just eight months older than Donald Jr., and they
grew up together. Wayne's dad and I are best friends, and Wayne has
always referred to me as "Uncle Donald." By his own admission,
Wayne had no idea that Donald Jr. had a disability until his father
told him at about the age of twelve. "I just assumed he was quirky,"
Wayne says. "When we were little he was vivacious and talkative just
like everyone else . . . then his anxiety grew as he got older."

Despite Donald Jr.'s increasing anxiety, it would never have
occurred to Wayne to exclude him. "For him, and for my friends,
it was a good thing. My friends had the chance to see Donald Jr. as
something other than 'just weird,' and they really put the effort in to
get to know him and draw him out. And for Donald Jr., it was a growth
thing—it took him some time to open up to them, but the more he
was around my friends, the more comfortable he got over time."

When asked to give his advice on making friends with someone
with ID, Wayne said, "You just have to get your foot in the door and
jump headfirst into it. It's like with anyone else—you figure out who
the person is and what their interests are, and they will just open up to
it." Wayne admits it can be challenging and that many people avoid
the issue entirely because they find it too awkward. "It is incredibly
difficult to maintain a conversation with Donald Jr. You have to know
how to steer the conversation and just push through it." In the end,

65

Wayne says, you just accept them for who they are. "It's not a big deal for us . . . Donald Jr.'s just one of the guys."

Ty Ruun

Excerpted from an informational piece Ty wrote
for me after his year with Donald Jr.

I am Ty Ruun, and I lived with Donald Jr. in 2008-2009. Living with Donald Jr. is both challenging and rewarding. Donald Jr. is a special person. But you have to keep in mind that he is both special *and* a person. By this I mean he is a human being; he has the same feelings, emotions, wants, and needs as everyone else. He is perfectly capable of having a conversation, getting his own food, and taking care of himself. So you don't have to baby him.

That being said, he is special. You still have to look after him, make sure he's on top of things, and spend more time with him to ensure that he is taking care of business. I went back and forth between being too much on top of him and giving him too much leeway to where he would mess things up. It will take time to find a happy medium, but just be patient with it.

You're in college, which is awesome, so enjoy it. Have fun. Donald Jr. likes to relax and have fun, occasionally sit around and do nothing just like everyone else. You don't have to be on top of him 24/7. It shouldn't be a burden. In fact, it enhanced my year, as I viewed him as my friend.

Living with Donald Jr. can be a challenge. Many college students have a tough time looking after themselves, let alone another person. Just keep in mind you are doing something important. I was second in command of the Navy ROTC in charge of the PSA and took thirty-six hours of classes, and I was still able to spend ample time with Donald Jr. Live your life, go out of town for the weekend—have fun!

Request for Proposal (RFP)

CTC
College Transition Connection, Inc.
Partnership Project

Transition and Postsecondary Education Program Grant

Request for Proposals
2009

APPLICATION DATES AND DEADLINES

Application Deadline ....September 15, 2009
Grant Awarded ....October 15 – November 1, 2009
First Installment ....November 1, 2009
Second Installment ....Disbursed June 1, 2010
Third Installment.........................Disbursed June 1, 2011

Donald Bailey

June 10, 2009

Dear Colleagues:

The College Transition Connection, Inc. is pleased to announce that grant applications are being accepted for an inclusive model Transition and Postsecondary Education Program sponsored by the College Transition Connection (CTC)—formerly Charleston Transition College. This grant will award planning and seed funds to an institution of higher education in South Carolina for the development of a postsecondary education program for students with intellectual disabilities.

This grant will be for $55,000 for a planning period from November 1, 2009 through May 31, 2010. The planning grant will provide an opportunity to develop the program, establish active partnerships and operational plans, and recruit a first class of 6-8 students so that the program can begin in August/September 2010. Following the successful completion of the planning period, program seed funding will be available for two additional years. CTC has established a Task Force of professionals, parents, and others who have extensive knowledge of postsecondary education and students with intellectual disabilities. Through research of existing programs and deliberations, this Task Force has developed guidelines to assist in the development of a successful postsecondary education model program.

Please note that completed applications must be received by September 15, 2009. One original and two copies should be mailed to Donald Bailey at P.O. Box 31656, Charleston, SC, 29417. Please direct any questions regarding grant preparation to Mr. Bailey at 1-843-763-4169.

We look forward to your response.

Donald Bailey
Chairman and CEO, College Transition Connection

College Transition Connection, Inc. (CTC)—formerly Charleston Transition College

CTC was formed by parents and professionals in the Southeast United States to develop opportunities for transition to independent living for students and young adults with intellectual disabilities, including the development of postsecondary, life-long learning, employment, social, and independent and supported living options. The CTC Board has raised substantial funds to accomplish these goals and has developed partnerships with key organizations and agencies in the state.

The interest of CTC and its constituents is driven by many factors. First, studies have shown students with intellectual disabilities that participate in postsecondary education are more likely to excel in academics, employment, and life. Second, many children with intellectual disabilities are now being included in K-12 and want to pursue postsecondary education like their peers and siblings.

CTC/NDSS Partnership Project

The College Transition Connection, Inc. and the National Down Syndrome Society have developed a partnership project to create a high-quality, inclusive model postsecondary program at a two- or four-year college or university in South Carolina. The goal of this partnership project is to support the development of a program that will offer excellent postsecondary educational opportunities for students with intellectual disabilities and be self-sustaining after a planning period and two years of subsequent funding. The desired outcomes of the transition and postsecondary program* are academic enrichment, socialization, independent living skills, and competitive or supported employment.

---

* From here on, wherever postsecondary is mentioned, this should be interpreted as transition and postsecondary.

Donald Bailey

Grant Parameters

Fifty-five thousand dollars will be awarded for a planning period to develop a postsecondary program. The grant for the planning period will be from November 1, 2009, through May 31, 2010. During this time, the grantee will use the funds to develop the program; establish active partnerships with local school district(s) and other adult service agencies; and create an operational plan so that the program is ready to launch at the end of the planning period grant. Students will apply and be admitted to the program, and will participate in orientation to both the institution of higher education and to the program, prior to the beginning of the school term in the Fall of 2010.

Additional funds of up to $50,000 per year will be available for the first two operational years of the program, dependent on the successful outcome of the planning year. Total funds for this pilot program, including the planning year, will not exceed $155,000. The program must be sustainable without any additional funds from CTC upon the completion of the second operational year. It is important that the plan for sustainability be addressed in this grant proposal.

Eligible Applicants

The grant is open to institutions of higher education in South Carolina. The ideal applicant is a consortium of institutions of higher education and school district(s), as well as community and adult service providers. In the case of a consortium, the lead applicant must be an institution of higher education. Each lead applicant should choose a Program Director, who will be the primary contact for the institution of higher education and/or the consortium of active partners during the grant application process.

CTC/NDSS Postsecondary Education Task Force

CTC and NDSS established a Task Force of experts from a diverse representation of key stakeholders from South Carolina and the

Southeast (e.g., families, individuals with disabilities, educators, state agency administrators) who have extensive knowledge of transition and postsecondary education and students with intellectual disabilities. This Task Force developed strong guidelines to follow in developing a model postsecondary program and identified certain components that should be included in a postsecondary program to ensure successful student outcomes.

Task Force Recommendations

Included below are some of the guidelines/recommendations of the Task Force. The guidelines established by the Task Force will give the chosen institution(s) a foundation from which to build their program.

- The Task Force hopes that a postsecondary experience will help these students obtain the desire and habits to become life-long learners. The Task Force recommends that the institution of higher education address ways that life-long learning can be addressed and how the institution of higher education would provide students opportunities to take courses in the future, after the completion of the program.
- The first class should have approximately 6-8 students, with expansion of the number of students as the program grows.
- A mix of credit and noncredit classes should be offered. There should be three possibilities for coursework available: (1) small group (noncredit) special education classes (2) inclusion in regular classes for credit, if appropriate for the individual student, and (3) inclusion in regular classes without earning credit (auditing the classes). Support should be provided (e.g., through an educational coach, peer mentor, or technology) when a student participates in a credit (regular) class.
- While the majority of students in the program will not be seeking a degree, they should receive a certificate of program completion from the institution of higher education.
- The length of the postsecondary program should be at least two years.

- The Task Force felt that a strong asset to a postsecondary program could be a residential component, while recognizing that such a component would be difficult to implement from the beginning. The proposal should include information about the ability of the school to include this component. Preference will be given to applications that include planning for a residential component; however a residential component is not required.

Proposal Requirements

The proposal should be a detailed narrative of how your institution of higher education and/or consortium of active partners will establish the program. The proposal should be approached as a detailed outline of how your program will be designed, how it will address the major elements outlined by the Task Force within the planning period, and how it will be implemented. The description of the planning period should describe how you will initiate the ideas and processes included in your proposal, including establishing partnerships (if not already formed), finding funding sources, and obtaining the necessary state approval(s), if any. Technical assistance will be available throughout the project to assist with: strategic planning; developing partnerships; identifying best practice; and providing expertise and assistance as needed. Please follow the Proposal Outline below.

Proposals that demonstrate active partnerships with other institutions of higher education, school district(s) and/or adult/ community service providers will be looked upon favorably. The proposal submitted should specifically reflect how the partner(s) will work together in this program. It would be in the best interest of all applicants to incorporate the Task Force guidelines into their proposals and/or discuss why they chose a different route on particular components.

Proposal Outline

1. Need (5 points)

    - Why is postsecondary education important for individuals with intellectual disabilities?
    - Particularly reference why your school or consortium believes that a postsecondary program fits into the mission of the school(s).

2. Program Design (45)

    - How will you address the need(s) identified in Number 1?
    - Discuss if this project will be a collaborative effort, and if so, discuss the active partners who will collaborate (institutions of higher education, school district(s), and/ or adult/community service agencies) and their unique responsibilities
    - Include discussion about ways to coordinate schedules of school district(s) with those of the colleges for those students who might be dually enrolled.
    - Discuss ways to achieve desired outcomes:

        • Academic Enrichment: Curriculum (what will be included and why—math, reading, etc.), method of delivery, location of services, etc. Describe inclusive academic opportunities as well as remedial options.
        • Socialization: What will be done to foster socialization and camaraderie among students, the college, and the community? How will peer mentors be involved in the program?
        • Independent Living Skills: Discussion should include curriculum (how these skills will be taught), method of delivery, and location of services. Teaching of self-determination and self-advocacy skills should also be addressed in this section.

- Competitive or Supported Employment: Program should include training that will result in long-term employment upon completion of the program. Students will participate in paid and/or unpaid employment experiences during the program, which might include internships or positions on or off-campus.

- Discuss your vision of what courses, services, etc. will be offered/required of every student and how the program will be individualized to a student's specific needs.
- Include information about the guidelines discussed above and address the following issues:

  - Length of program: number of years, why?
  - Number of students: Discuss the number of students who will be admitted the first and second year of the program. Keep in mind natural proportions when determining the number of students.
  - Credit/noncredit: Discuss the school(s)' willingness to accommodate both credit and noncredit courses and to accommodate students whose needs might fall outside the general parameters of the program—perhaps with special interests/career goals and/or ability to seek a degree.
  - Explain how there will be meaningful social and academic inclusion.

- Review the admissions criteria established by the Task Force and discuss ways these criteria will/will not work with your school's admissions criteria. Include any discussion of criteria that you agree/disagree with and why.
  Suggested admissions criteria:

  - Must be between 18-26 years old
  - Have an intellectual disability
  - Have demonstrated the ability to learn and participate in classroom and work settings

- Demonstrated interest and desire to pursue educational, employment, and life experiences through postsecondary education
- Agree to participate in an interview process
- Agree to actively participate in assessments, such as independent living and others
- Three letters of recommendation (excluding relatives)

3. Implementation Plan (30 points)

   - Include a discussion of goals, objectives, outcomes, and timelines for accomplishing tasks for the planning period, including on-going communication with a representative from CTC and regular meetings with the Task Force or Steering Committee of the Task Force.
   - Incorporate information about the active partnerships that are or will be established to form a consortium (e.g., institution of higher education, school district, adult service agency, community agencies, etc.), if a consortium is planned. With this, include detailed information about the roles and responsibilities, including financial, of all active partnerships.
   - Include discussion of plans to adequately research and obtain appropriate state approvals for this program (if any), which may differ for those who are dually enrolled (ages 18-21).
   - Include discussion about how institutions will meet with state agencies and CTC during the planning year to best accommodate students academically and financially. Some examples of agencies to be included in these discussions are South Carolina Department of Education, Vocational Rehabilitation Agency, and the Department of Disability and Special Needs (Note: this is not an all-inclusive list).
   - Outline how this project will be staffed.
   - Discuss ways of creatively staffing the program, both in the planning period and the operational years (e.g., hiring graduate students to assist with teaching courses

or organizing programs, recruiting college students as mentors and buddies for social or academic reasons, etc.).

- Organizational structure of the project (include a table of organization).
- Plan for continuous improvement and progress (project staff meetings, advisory committee, internal monitoring procedures).
- Discuss potential funding options for the program, including, but not limited to, public funding (IDEA, DDSN, VR, etc.) as well as other streams of funding (tuition, grants, etc.). Please specify projected tuition costs.
- Proposal must demonstrate definitively how the program will be sustainable without additional funds from CTC at the end of the third grant period. Include projection budgets for the first two operational years of the program

4. Evaluation Plan (20 points)

- Include a comprehensive evaluation plan that will include both qualitative and quantitative methodology over time. Also, include any research projects that would be part of the program design.
- Discuss quantitative methods to track student outcome including:

    • Academic Enrichment
    • Socialization
    • Independent Living Skills
    • Competitive or Supported Employment

- Discuss qualitative indicators measuring outcomes

    • Discuss qualitative indicators measuring outcomes that evaluate the strength of the program in the areas of academic enrichment, socialization, independent living skills, and competitive or supported employment

Application Guidelines for 2009

Please submit one original and four (2) copies of complete application, including attachments, to:

Donald Bailey
P.O. Box 31656
Charleston, SC 29417

APPLICATIONS MUST BE RECEIVED BY SEPTEMBER 15, 2009

All copies should be collated, and all attachments should include the Program Director's name and institution of higher education. If the proposal will involve multiple institutions, please be sure to indicate which institution will be administering the grant. Any questions regarding grant preparation should be referred to Donald Bailey at 1-843-763-4169.

Applications must include the following, in this order:

1. Letter of Intent—This letter should include background on the lead applicant; the mission of the school; why your institution has an interest in this program; brief summary of past programs/experience; and why you think your institution/ consortium would be able to successfully create a transition and postsecondary program for individuals with intellectual disabilities. Please limit the synopsis to one or two (1 or 2) typed page(s), single-sided, single-spaced, one-inch margins and minimum of 12-point font.
2. Detailed proposal following the Proposal Outline above. The length of this proposal should not exceed ten (10) typed, single-sided, single-spaced pages with one-inch margins and minimum of 12-point font.
3. Updated Curriculum Vitae (CV) for all known individuals who will be working on the program and information as to their role(s) in this project.

4. Annual Budget of proposed program—Include explanation of how the requested award would be used, in addition to any in-kind or matching contributions.

5. Letter of commitment—Include letters from all active partners that state their proposed role and responsibilities (including financial) in the partnership, their agreement to their role, and that they understand and support the program that is being proposed. This letter should be on letterhead and should be signed by the head of the institution/organization (i.e., institutions of higher education—President; school district(s)—Superintendent; service providers and others—Executive Director, etc.).

The review committee reserves the right to request additional information from the institution(s) of higher education and their active partners.

Application/Award Process

Applicants will be notified by e-mail as to the outcome of the grant. Site visits will be scheduled to meet with project leaders and other key personnel (i.e., President of the institution of higher education) and review the RFP. All publications resulting from work carried out during the term of the award must carry a statement of CTC support.

APPENDIX B

Donald A. Bailey's testimony before the SC General Assembly's Higher Education, Technical, and Cultural Subcommittee of the Ways and Means Committee on January 31, 2007

Mr. Chairman and members of the committee, thank you very much for this opportunity to speak with you today about an exciting new opportunity for students with disabilities in South Carolina. I am the chair of CTC [College Transition Connection], a nonprofit organization dedicated to expanding education, employment, and independent living opportunities for individuals with intellectual disabilities . . .

We have raised a total of $300,000 in donations and pledges of support, and we request $300,000 from the state to develop a model postsecondary program for students with intellectual disabilities. These are students with significant learning, cognitive or developmental disabilities, such as mental retardation. These students qualify for special education services until they turn age 22. However, they do not have the opportunity to participate in postsecondary education with students their own age where they can learn the social, academic, and vocational skills needed to be successfully employed and live independently.

What happens to these students after they leave school? According to a federal report, 92% are not employed. The cost to the taxpayer can be as much as one and a half million dollars for an unemployed individual with significant disabilities from age 22 to 65. Unemployment, long waiting lists for housing and employment supports, isolation, and living at home with aging parents are typical.

However, with education and the right support, these young people are very capable of learning, working, being a part of their communities, and becoming taxpaying citizens. A new wave of postsecondary programs is emerging for these students across the country. Currently there are over 110 such programs in 28 states. Research is showing that students who participate in these programs are much more likely to become employed, live independently, and participate in their communities.

CTC has formed a partnership with the National Down Syndrome Society (NDSS), an organization that is taking a leading role in supporting the development of these postsecondary programs. NDSS has helped to connect us to national experts who are providing technical expertise in developing a model program here in South Carolina.

NDSS and CTC have established a Task Force of distinguished experts, including parents, individuals with disabilities, institutions of higher education, educators, and state agency administrators who have extensive knowledge of transition and postsecondary education.

Our Task Force has created a partnership with three colleges in the Charleston area—the College of Charleston, Charleston Southern University, and Trident Technical College—and we are reaching out to other colleges in the state. We plan to develop a model pilot program. After two years of operation, the model program is anticipated to be self-sufficient through agency funding and tuition. Technical assistance material will be developed that will help other colleges in South Carolina develop similar programs.

After researching successful programs, this Task Force developed guidelines to follow in developing a model program. The program will include academic enrichment, independent living skills, socialization, opportunities to participate in extracurricular activities, and vocational experiences leading to competitive or supported employment. Students will participate in a mix of special classes and regular classes with support. Students will earn a certificate when they finish the program.

An exciting part of this project is the opportunity to help train future special and general education teachers. College graduate or undergraduate students majoring in education, special education, and related fields will participate as teaching assistants, peer mentors, job coaches or in other roles. This will be invaluable training.

The funds we are requesting from the state will support the development, start-up costs, and evaluation of the model program; development of technical assistance information for other colleges; and coordination among state and local agencies. We will also hold a Roundtable on Developing Postsecondary Programs for Students with Intellectual Disabilities. This roundtable will be jointly sponsored with the University of South Carolina Center for Excellence in Developmental Disabilities. This center, located in the University of South Carolina School of Medicine Center for Disability Resources, is partnering with CTC in this project. At the roundtable we will bring together key national experts with leaders in South Carolina higher education, state and local agencies, parent organizations, and students with disabilities. Highlights of successful programs, technical assistance in program development, and collaboration will be discussed.

In the attachments to my written testimony I have provided data, research, and background information that I hope will be helpful. Please let me know if you would like any additional information.

In conclusion, those of us who have children with disabilities want the same thing for our children as everyone else wants—the opportunity for them to be educated, to work, to have friends, and to live in the community. We ask for your support in making this possible. Thank you again for the opportunity to speak to you today.

APPENDIX C

School Program Descriptions

CarolinaLIFE Program at the University of South Carolina

The CarolinaLIFE Program is an innovative two- to four-year, postsecondary program at the University of South Carolina for students with intellectual or cognitive disabilities. CarolinaLIFE offers students with intellectual or cognitive disabilities the opportunity to experience college life through inclusive participation in academic, social, vocational, and independent living activities.

CarolinaLIFE students create their own unique academic experience and do not have a prescribed curriculum. During their first semester, CarolinaLIFE students participate in two to three hours of small-group instruction as they receive education in the skills necessary for college success. This includes content on campus orientation, campus electronic systems, and study skills. Students also attend an inclusive class, University 101, with incoming USC freshman.

During the first semester, students also connect with peer mentors and explore social activities and employment options. After the first semester, students spend more time in university courses and less time receiving support services.

CarolinaLIFE students are able to live with other typical USC students in the Cliff Apartments on Whaley Street.

All CarolinaLIFE students participate in an orientation session and benefit from individual planning, academic advisement and evaluation, peer mentoring, and access to assistive technology.

For more information, please visit
http://www.sa.sc.edu/carolinalife

Donald Bailey

ClemsonLIFE at Clemson University

The ClemsonLIFE program is a two- to three-year program at Clemson University for students with intellectual disabilities who desire a postsecondary experience on a college campus. ClemsonLIFE's mission is to provide a coordinated course of study that includes career exploration and preparation along with self-awareness, discovery, and personal improvement though a framework of courses, job internships, and community participation.

ClemsonLIFE students take classes in applied math, personal fitness, literature, career skills, and communication. Students also learn from their involvement in a job or internship.

Students are placed into supervised jobs on campus for the first two semesters and then move into more independent placements off campus the final two semesters.

During his or her employment, each student develops an electronic employment portfolio to present to prospective employers upon completion of the program. This portfolio contains videos from job placement experiences along with other artifacts, giving potential employers a complete picture of what the student is capable of doing.

Students live in an on-campus apartment for the first two semesters and off campus for the final two semesters. Groups of three ClemsonLIFE students live with one residence supervisor. Residence supervisors observe students and track their progress in developing independent living skills. Daytime and evening activities are planned for the students.

Mentors from Clemson's traditional student population assist ClemsonLIFE students as academic tutors, job coaches, resident supervisors, and class supervisors. They also serve as buddies for meals, fitness workouts, and social activities. These mentors help ClemsonLIFE students unlock and achieve their potential and prepare them for independent living.

For more information, please visit
http://www.clemson.edu/culife

LIFE Program at Coastal Carolina University

Coastal Carolina University's LIFE program is a four-year postsecondary education program for students with intellectual disabilities. The purpose of the program is to promote a smooth and effective transition from secondary schools to a four-year higher-education institution, as well as provide postsecondary opportunities on a college campus.

The LIFE program provides vocational evaluation that includes academic and job skill counseling, testing, and on-the-job evaluations to help students learn about and identify the types of jobs/careers they are most interested in pursuing.

The LIFE program also identifies and develops an individualized career plan that will enable students, upon completion of the program, to be able to 1) pursue and obtain employment of choice in their field of interest; 2) develop work skills necessary to function successfully within the working environment; 3) develop socialization skills; and 4) build or enhance basic academic skills in areas of need/interest.

Students participate in internships on and off campus.

The LIFE program assists students in developing life skills required to live independently within the local community and provides positive social experiences to prepare students for various life experiences. The LIFE program uses assistive technology to facilitate academic, vocational, and communication goals.

For more information, please visit
http://www.coastal.edu/education/LIFE

REACH Program at the College of Charleston

The REACH (Realizing Educational and Career Hopes) Program at the College of Charleston is a four-year, inclusive, non-degree-seeking program for students with mild to moderate intellectual disabilities. The purpose of the program is to provide the opportunity for all students to realize their intellectual and personal potential and to become responsible, productive members of society. REACH students participate in the academic, residential, social, and cultural experiences offered by the College, with appropriate support for success.

REACH students have the option of living with other REACH students and traditional College of Charleston students in the REACH house on Coming Street. The REACH house features an undergraduate residential advisor as well as a graduate assistant who provides additional support and help for weekend plans and travel. Basic life skills, such as nutrition and personal finance, are taught on site.

All REACH students interact with academic mentors, social mentors, and housemates from the College's traditional student population. Additionally, all REACH students benefit from life-skills training and career development services, which includes a seminar on workplace success and placement in work-study programs or internships.

For more information, please visit
http://reach.cofc.edu

Winthrop Transition to College at Winthrop University

The mission of the Winthrop Transition to College Program is to provide postsecondary options for students with intellectual disabilities. In collaboration with the Fort Mill and Rock Hill school districts, the WTC Program provides access to instruction in academics, employment, recreation, community-based activities, and functional, independent living for transition-age students with intellectual disabilities. This program serves six to eight students, ages eighteen to twenty-one, in a mixed curriculum that includes classes focused on independent living, academic skills, and campus employment.

WTC students attend a number of selected courses and are employed on campus in a variety of settings.

WTC students are paired with traditional student mentors. In turn, these mentors receive guidance and support from the Winthrop Transition to College program coordinator and high school personnel.

For more information, please visit
http://www2.winthrop.edu/transitioncollege

APPENDIX D

Websites of Interest

College Transition Connection
http://collegetransitionconnection.org/

University of South Carolina LIFE
http://www.sa.sc.edu/carolinalife/

Clemson LIFE
http://www.clemson.edu/culife/

Coastal Carolina LIFE
http://www.coastal.edu/education/LIFE/

Winthrop Transition College
http://www2.winthrop.edu/transitioncollege/

College of Charleston REACH Program
http://reach.cofc.edu/

Think College
http://www.thinkcollege.net/

Transition to College
http://www.transitiontocollege.net/

Vocational Rehabilitation—State Offices
https://askjan.org/cgi-win/TypeQuery.exe?902

Donald Bailey

National Down Syndrome Society
http://www.ndss.org/

Autism Society
http://www.autism-society.org/

American Association on Intellectual and Developmental Disabilities
http://www.aamr.org/

Division on Developmental Disabilities
http://daddcec.org/Home.aspx

Institute for Inclusion
http://www.instituteforinclusion.org/

Institute for Community Inclusion
http://www.communityinclusion.org/

ABOUT THE AUTHOR

Donald Bailey is a lifelong resident of Charleston, South Carolina. He and his wife, Caroline, have two children and three grandchildren. His younger child has cognitive learning difficulties. Bailey is a founding chairman of the Charleston Transition College and now serves as executive director.

31578806R00068

Made in the USA
San Bernardino, CA
05 April 2019